The Best
Men's Stage Monologues
# of 1994

Smith and Kraus *Books For Actors*
THE MONOLOGUE SERIES

> The Best Men's / Women's Stage Monologues of 1992
> The Best Men's / Women's Stage Monologues of 1991
> The Best Men's / Women's Stage Monologues of 1990
> One Hundred Men's / Women's Stage Monologues from the 1980's
> 2 Minutes and Under: Character Monologues for Actors
> Street Talk: Character Monologues for Actors
> Uptown: Character Monologues for Actors
> Monologues from Contemporary Literature: Volume I
> Monologues from Classic Plays
> 100 Great Monologues from the Renaissance Theatre
> 100 Great Monologues from the Neo-Classical Theatre
> 100 Great Monologues from the 19th C. Romantic and Realistic Theatres

FESTIVAL MONOLOGUE SERIES

> The Great Monologues from the Humana Festival
> The Great Monologues from the EST Marathon
> The Great Monologues from the Women's Project
> The Great Monologues from the Mark Taper Forum

YOUNG ACTORS SERIES

> Great Scenes and Monologues for Children
> New Plays from A.C.T.'s Young Conservatory
> Great Scenes for Young Actors from the Stage
> Great Monologues for Young Actors
> Multicultural Monologues for Young Actors
> Multicultural Scenes for Young Actors

SCENE STUDY SERIES

> Scenes From Classic Plays 468 B.C. to 1960 A.D.
> The Best Stage Scenes of 1993
> The Best Stage Scenes of 1992
> The Best Stage Scenes for Men / Women from the 1980's

CONTEMPORARY PLAYWRIGHTS SERIES

> Romulus Linney: 17 Short Plays
> Eric Overmyer: Collected Plays
> Lanford Wilson: 21 Short Plays
> William Mastrosimone: Collected Plays
> Horton Foote: 4 New Plays
> Israel Horovitz: 16 Short Plays
> Terrence McNally: 15 Short Plays
> Humana Festival '93: The Complete Plays
> Humana Festival '94: The Complete Plays
> Women Playwrights: The Best Plays of 1992
> Women Playwrights: The Best Plays of 1993

GREAT TRANSLATION FOR ACTORS SERIES

> The Wood Demon by Anton Chekhov

CAREER DEVELOPMENT SERIES

> The Camera Smart Actor
> The Sanford Meisner Approach
> The Actor's Chekhov
> Kiss and Tell: Restoration Scenes, Monologues, & History
> Cold Readings: Some Do's and Don'ts for Actors at Auditions

If you require pre-publication information about upcoming Smith and Kraus books, you may receive our semi-annual catalogue, free of charge, by sending your name and address to *Smith and Kraus Catalogue, P.O. Box 127, One Main Street, Lyme, NH 03768. Or call us at (800) 895-4331, fax (603) 795-4427.*

The Best
Men's Stage Monologues
of 1994

edited by Jocelyn A. Beard

The Monologue Audition Series

SK
A Smith and Kraus Book

Published by Smith and Kraus, Inc.
One Main Street, Lyme, NH 03768

First Edition: November 1994
10 9 8 7 6 5 4 3 2 1

The Monologue Audition Series ISSN 1067-134X

NOTE: These monologues are intended to be used for audition and class study; permission is not required to use the material for those purposes. However, if there is a paid performance of any of the monologues included in this book, please refer to the permissions acknowledgment pages to locate the source who can grant permission for public performance.

Contents

Preface

Men, men, men, men…no, it's not a Monty Python song, it's the 1994 theatrical season! Do we have some men for you this year, or what!? From the tyrannical patriarch of THE KENTUCKY CYCLE to doomed Jason in Alistair Elliot's sizzling new translation of MEDEA, the men of 1994 are an amazing lot. I know you'll probably think I'm pandering to you in a thinly disguised effort to convince you to buy this book (or to make you feel great about having already done so) but when I took a look at the male roles this year, I began to harbor for the first time ever a secret desire to be able to change my sex, if only for a little while, so that I, too, could tackle some of these phenomenal characters. Do you guys realize how lucky you are? After all, when do we gals have the opportunity to play a hunchback addicted to pain pills (MAMBO QUASIMODO)? Or a Cambodian doctor struggling to survive in the Killing Fields (THE SURVIVOR: A CAMBODIAN ODYSSEY)? Or better yet, the man himself: Oscar Wilde (STEPHEN AND MR. WILDE)? The answer is: rarely. Oh, I'm not complaining. The women's roles this season are equally spectacular, but once—just once— I'd love to be able to play Jason instead of Medea. Oh, I know: Medea gets to fly from the palace rooftop in a winged chariot, but Jason gets to stay and grieve. But I digress…

You simply can't go wrong with a season that includes work from the likes of Tom Stoppard, Gloria Naylor, Richard Nelson, Harold Pinter, Terrence McNally and Tony Kushner. They're all in here, as well as a host of exciting new voices from both here and abroad who have created fascinating characters whose prime words—their monologues—are collected for you in this book. There are monologues from one-man shows, like Leslie Jordan's HYSTERICAL BLINDNESS and from street-wise ensemble pieces like Marion McClinton's POLICE BOYS. In this collection you will find a televangelist, a dying man, an Ambassador trying to hide his sexuality, a psychiatrist who specializes in reintegrating multiple personalities, a police captain retiring after 30 years on the force, a southern slave plotting a rebellion and a man who thinks nothing of kidnapping a women and hobbling her in order to keep her as his wife. And that's just the beginning! My advice: start reading!

(I'm so jealous!) Break a leg!

—*Jocelyn A. Beard*
Patterson, NY
Autumn, 1994

I would like to dedicate this book to my favorite male character: Sean G. Bagley—of the Pumpkin Hill Bagleys.

Introduction

No matter what you're looking for, as long as it can be expressed by one person, there's plenty here to choose from, and plenty here to challenge you. These monologues for male characters have been masterfully excerpted from recent works by some of Britain's, America's, and even Russia's most interesting dramatists. There are pieces here penned by Pulitzer, Tony, and Olivier Award-winners, as well as by writers whose names you may not have heard before, but you will again soon, I promise. There are selections here first spoken in London's West End, on Broadway, at America's regional theaters, and by experimental troupes. The spectrum of style and subject matter puts me in mind of Polonius cataloguing dramatic genres for the Prince of Denmark. There are monologues political, lyrical, humorous, supernatural, historical, lyrical-political, historical-humorous, and every other hybrid possible. It is diversity in ten dimensions, and for my money that makes this a treasury worth having on a shelf close at hand.

These pages also proudly proclaim what's this and here and now in the act of dramatic writing. While that alone deserves the attention of anyone who considers her or himself a theatre aficionado, it has a special value for actors and playwrights. Whether in training or already working in the profession, actors who rely on this book as a source for assignments and auditions can rest assured that directors, teachers, and agents haven't already heard them a zillion times. Consequently, rather than tune out when your turn comes, the very people you want to impress are more likely to tune in. Once they do, you've got them where they'd really rather be—absorbed in what you're up to on the stage. Emerging playwrights, furthermore, would do well to master this basic building block of dramaturgy, since significant new plays are being conceived, written, and produced in monologue form (Brian Friel's *Faith Healer*, Spalding Gray's *Gray's Anatomy*, and Jon Robin Baitz's *Three Hotels*, to name a few). By anatomizing these pages, observant young writers can glean some rules of the monologue game—and then discover how best to break them.

I value this assemblage of monologues, too, because it represents a time capsule for the theatre's social, political, and aesthetic concerns of 1994. As such, it holds great promise for the future, and forecasters of theatrical doom and gloom will just have to step aside while we celebrate the impressive array of passion, imagination, and verbal acuity on display in this collection. No matter how you read these pages—cover to cover or only a monologue a month—you'll encounter here a group of playwrights talented and brave enough to address the overwhelming problems of the day while pushing us to the edge of tomorrow. So read on and discover who's leading this grand old theatre into the 21st century—not just alive, but kicking!

Michael Bigelow Dixon
Literary Manager
Actors Theatre of Louisville

The Best
Men's Stage Monologues
of 1994

Alchemy of Desire/
Dead-Man's Blues
Caridad Svich

Scene: An open, fluid space evocative of a burnt-out bayou, the present
Dramatic
    Jamie: a young man killed in battle, 20-30

Here, a restless young spirit tries to come to terms with his life and death while experiencing the wounds that killed him.

JAMIE: Oh – I got beat up bad.
Those bullets went right through me.
Got holes all over: arms, chest, thigh . . .
Even my damn breathin's screwed up.
(*Breathes audibly.*) Hear that?
It's like I got no air goin' into my throat.
Bullets wiped me clean, clean out of air.
Damn blood and holes and . . .
Can't feel my dick.
Can't feel your dick, you ain't a man, right?
I don't even know where I am. Nothin' looks familiar.
Spooky.

I was doin' good, too.
I was beatin' up the bad guys left and right
jumpin' on 'em like –
WISH TO HELL I knew where I am.
Feels like I'm all alone on the earth:
alone, and stinkin'.

Got somethin'. Got some – air – left.
Cracked . . .

I'd get to feel this way – before – yeh –
take out this picture.

(*Takes photograph out of pocket.*)

GODDAM BLOOD's right cross it.
(*Scraping blood off picture.*) Gets hard, blood . . .
There. Can sorta see it.
Yeh. That's her. That's . . . Simone.

Oh, I got lots of girls, but she's the one I married.
Yeh. I married her.
Nobody believed it when I did it.
"Man, what you doin' gettin' married for," they said,
"You got it perfect. Why you go have to ruin it?"
Don't know. Just felt right.
Looked at her one day and I thought,
"I'll marry this one."

It was like she was in my skin.
Like she'd been in my skin for years
even though I'd only just met her.
"I'll marry this one,"
'For to desire and to be desired is better than to BURN.'"

(*Sound of plane flying in the distance.*)

Head's startin' to hurt.
That's no good.
NO . . .

(*Fade.*)

I married her.

She was so sad when I left.
I was goin' out on that bus to here,

and she just kept lookin' at me. Like I did somethin'.

"WHAT THE HELL is she sad about?" I thought,
"I'm the one who's leavin'. I'm the one goin' God knows where
to get God knows beat up so bad I can't even breathe."

But she just kept standin' there on the side of the road,
the bus drivin' off and all I could see was her
standin' there on the side of the road with those eyes . . .
and then nothin'.

(*Sound: very faint thunder. Fade.*)

'Cept for this picture.
And she don't even look that good in it:
her mouth's all crooked
eyes kinda cross-eyed –
SHE DON'T LOOK GOOD AT ALL.

(*Pause.*)

dear Simone . . .
I am beat up.
I am beat up bad.

(*Blackout.*)

Allen, Naked
Robert Coles

Scene: Here and now
Serio-Comic
    Irv: a man who likes volleyball, 20s

    Here, Irv introduces himself to the audience with a slightly obsessive tale of one of his volleyball teammates.

O   O   O

IRV: I'm Irv. Short for Irving. You've got to be a really old Jew to name your kid Irving in the second half of the 20th century. But that was my father, all right. An old Jew. A good Jew. I work for an insurance company. No, I don't sell it. Everyone seems to think an insurance company consists only of agents. I work in the home office, but don't ask what I do because it makes even *my* eyes glaze over to explain it. And I don't do a whole lot for fun, either, except one thing: volleyball. No, not on the beach. Your exposure to the sport might be limited to slapping a ball around underhanded on the sand, or maybe the company picnic where everybody plays with a beer in one fist. But we play indoors. Six-man, USVBA rules. And we're good. Real good. I'm the setter. That means when the ball comes over to our side of the net, someone passes it to me and I toss it in the air so the hitter can hit it. That makes it sound a lot easier than it is. It's not easy. It's intricate, precise, elegant, graceful, lightning-fast, explosive, muscular and yet cerebral. To be a setter, one has to enter a virtual zen-like state of being. Almost a trance, but with total mental control. Complete relaxation, but with the instantaneous ability to react, to decide on a course of action without thinking. From a disaster – a ball passed four feet off course at knee level – one must, unconsciously, not only dig it, but *set* it, a soft but true arc, floating, without rotation, most likely backwards over one's head to the outside hitter, but executed in a manner that makes it clear to him that he's being set while utterly deceiving your opponents. That's the setter's job. And yet while you're in that zone, that state of grace, while *you* are utterly in command, your work seems effortless to the casual viewer. The warriors, the heroes, the Greek gods, the animals, the great golden beasts of the court are the hitters. They leap, they burst, they fly, they hang suspended above you like panthers about to pounce upon their prey. Then pow! They explode, the ball slamming straight down into the floor. The crowd roars – for *them,* not the setter. But they do deserve it, those great leaping animals. And there was no greater, no sleeker, no more golden god than Allen. Yes, a panther, a leopard, a lion, every big cat rolled into one. Now – God's truth – I'm straight. Yeah, I know you don't believe it. But, swear to God, I am. Man, my father's rolling over in his grave right now, I said "God" twice. He always would say to me, "Irving, Jews don't use that word. We don't take his name in vain." I would say, "Dad, God is not his name, it's his occupation. His name is Yahweh." Then he'd *really* go ballistic. Boy, I just said "God" four times and "Yahweh" once, that whole cemetery is probably rockin' right now. Anyway, I never had a gay thought in my life, and I'd seen Allen in gym shorts a hundred times, but that day in the locker room when he stood before me naked for the first time, something took place. In that single moment I found . . . not my sexuality . . . not . . . I don't honestly feel that anything was changed inside of me, just that I found something. I found . . . . . . Allen. And I felt I couldn't give up . . . . . . him. Allen. I couldn't give up the feeling that I had in that moment. And I tried to hold onto that feeling. And I did, as long as I was with Allen. And though we did . . . once . . . do . . . have . . . sex, I guess . . . it wasn't *that,* exactly. The feeling wasn't just that. Because we did . . . that . . . only once. But I had the feeling always with him. And the feeling was more than that. I swear. God's truth.

Arcadia
Tom Stoppard

Scene: A large country house in Derbyshire
Serio-Comic
  Valentine Coverly: a man enjoying a romance with mathematics, 25-30

When a visiting scholar discovers an iterated algorithm in the school work of a young girl who lived in his home some 180 years ago, Valentine does his best to explain the special significance of such a discovery. Here, he reveals his love of the mystery of creation, which he understands in purely mathematical terms.

O   O   O

VALENTINE: If you knew the algorithm and fed it back say ten thousand times, each time there'd be a dot somewhere on the screen. You'd never know where to expect the next dot. But gradually you'd start to see this shape, because every dot will be inside the shape of this leaf. It wouldn't *be* a leaf, it would be a mathematical object. But yes. The unpredictable and the predetermined unfold together to make everything the way it is. It's how nature creates itself, on every scale, the snowflake and the snowstorm. It makes me so happy. To be at the beginning again, knowing almost nothing. People were talking about the end of physics. Relativity and quantum looked as if they were going to clean out the whole problem between them. A theory of everything. But they only explained the very big and the very small. The universe, the elementary particles. The ordinary-sized stuff which is our lives, the things people write poetry about – clouds – daffodils – waterfalls – and what happens in a cup of coffee when the cream goes in – these things are full of mystery, as mysterious to us as the heavens were to the Greeks. We're better at predicting events at the edge of the galaxy or inside the nucleus of an atom than whether it'll rain on auntie's garden party three Sundays from now. Because the problem turns out to be different. We can't even predict the next drip from a dripping tap when it gets irregular. Each drip sets up the conditions for the next, the smallest variation blows prediction apart, and the weather is unpredictable the same way, will always be unpredictable. When you push the numbers through the computer you can see it on the screen. The future is disorder. A door like this has cracked open five or six times since we got up on our hind legs. It's the best possible time to be alive, when almost everything you thought you knew is wrong.

*

Arthur and Leila

Cherylene Lee

Scene: LA
Serio-Comic
   Arthur: Chinese-American, 64

Arthur is an alcoholic who has been selling pieces of junk to his sister and telling her that they are valuable family heirlooms. Arthur and Leila usually meet in the park for their exchanges, and here, the pigeons that patrol the ground nearby remind Arthur of the birds that they used to keep on the roof when they were children.

O   O   O

ARTHUR: Sometimes when I sit in this park, I think I see the old pigeons that we kept on papa's roof. Remember how I would feed them, take care of them all? So mama could make papa's favorite dish – roast squab.

[LEILA: The Kwan Yin carved from ivory. The teakwood chest in the center of the store –]

ARTHUR: I let some of the pigeons escape you know. I didn't want them all turned into dinner. There was one that cooed before I fed her. She was a beauty, very dignified. Never sat in her own shit.

[LEILA: Lanterns hanging from the ceiling, the laughing porcelain Buddha.]

ARTHUR: Fluffing up her feathers, making herself look bigger than she was. But she was very affectionate. Never pecked too hard. I named her after you, Lau Lan, Little Violet.

[LEILA: You always could spot a pigeon.]

ARTHUR: I let her go, you know, but she always came back. No matter what I did to shoo her away. Strange, isn't it? That instinct. Always coming back. (*Arthur moves away from the bench.*) I even thought I saw her the other day. Over by those other benches, where that old man is feeding birds. Doesn't she look like Lau Lan? Still the same after all these years. Amazing, eh? (*Liela has left. Arthur is alone, but continues as if Leila were there.*) Remember how I taught you to use Chinese soup spoons? You

8

asked me why there was that dip in the handle. I told you to fill up the fat spoon end, put the skinny end to your lips, then tip your head back so all the soup ran down the trough. It made papa so mad when you did that. Quai nui. Chinese girls didn't eat soup like that. He gave you a ling kwok on the side of the head. After that you called it a gutter spoon. You didn't like to use them anymore. You wanted American spoons, metal ones that burned your mouth when you put them into hot soup. Chinese spoons are better. Makes everything easier to swallow. Didn't I teach you that? (*Arthur smiles at the memory and sits on the bench alone. Lights fade.*)

Arthur and Leila

Cherylene Lee

Scene: LA
Dramatic
    Arthur: Chinese-American, 64

Leila is desperate for her brother to seek help for his drinking and gambling. When she presents him with the business card of a highly-recommended therapist, Arthur demands that they engage in a role-playing game in which Liela is Arthur and Arthur is the doctor. The game turns serious when Arthur, as the doctor, reveals his despair over his condition.

O   O   O

ARTHUR: (*Denial.*) You're not being honest with me. It isn't the loss that bothers you, is it? It's you. What you can't admit that you've done. Isn't that right . . . Mr. Chin? (*Beat.*) You know it wasn't your sister's fault. You have to admit you're a lousy gambler, a hopeless drunk, jui mow, that you've been a loser all your life. And after such high hopes. Your father, who worked so hard to send you to China, you not only ruined his business, you let him be humiliated, saw him sacrifice his face for you. You can't admit you disgraced your dead mother, your dead father. You let down the family, the community, Chinese civilization, a heritage of 5000 years. You who had so much to be proud of. No wonder your sister is ashamed. You have to accept that you wasted your life. You are a worthless man. Admit it. Because unless you give up your protection, your ridiculous Chinese pride, unless you stop hiding behind your inscrutable face, you will never be cured. You will die alone, penniless. No respect. You don't fit. You have never fit. So say it. Lose your face. Not the one you can buy, but the one that is inside. Ask me for help. Go on, ask. Better yet, beg. It's only when you have nothing. Nothing left of any value, when you are stripped naked of even your face – then maybe I can help. It won't cost much. It's cheap. You could become an honest man, sober, free, decent. No more pai gow, no more Wah Mei club. You could go to MacDonald's, watch TV. You could be nice, respectable, hardworking. Silent – like your father. (*Pause.*) Admit it, go on. Say it. Ask, Mr. Chin. Ask for my help.

Bailey's Cafe
Gloria Naylor

Scene: A narrow street that clings to the end of the world on a barren strip of earth.
   World time: 1948
Serio-Comic
   Sugar Man: smooth and smart; an astute observer of people's lives, 30-50

Sugar Man is as street smart as they come. Here, he shares a tale with an important message.

O   O   O

SUGAR MAN: The smoothest hustler I ever knew was a man by the name of Connie Mack. A New York hustler, so they don't come any greater than that.
[BAILEY: You want carrots?]
SUGAR MAN: Yeah, I want carrots. And double my boiled potatoes. (*To Maple.*) Now, Connie always went top shelf with his cars, *loved* driving new Cadillacs – he just didn't like to buy 'em. So here we go one day, cruising along, on a fine set of wheels that he'd happen to "borrow" from a gambler we called Black Jack. We're sitting on leather soft as butter, the engine purring, the radio blasting, and go to pull up to a light. And into the window comes the barrel of a loaded forty-five. Being held by one very angry man. You ever look up into the barrel of a cocked forty-five? Good – you don't wanna. And Black Jack goes, Hey, Connie, man, I told you I would kill your sorry ass if you ever messed with my car. And I'm gonna waste your buddy here – just for good measure. Now me – I ain't gonna lie – I was ready to start pleading for my life. But Connie never even breathed hard. He said, Black Jack are you crazy, man? – you think you the only Negro in New York who can own a purple Cadillac, with white leather seats, and the letters, B. J. painted on the side? I understand if you're upset cause you paid out all that money, thinking you were gonna get something special. But let's go beat up the dealer for selling us the same car.(*A beat.*) My point, chump, is that even when you find

your ass backed up to the ends of the earth – there's a way to improvise.

Before It Hits Home
Cheryl L. West

Scene: Here and now
Dramatic
> Wendal: a Black jazz musician with AIDS, 30s

> *After a difficult bout in the hospital, Wendal returns to his parents home where he hopes to find the strength to fight his illness. When his mother discovers that he has AIDS, she flies into a rage and demands that he pray to God for forgiveness. Here, Wendal reacts to his mother's condemnation with anger and frustration.*

○   ○   ○

WENDAL: Pray! Mama, what in the hell you think I've been doing? I've prayed every night. I laid in that hospital bed thirty-two days and thirty two nights and all I did was pray. You know how lonely it is Mama to lay in a bed that ain't even your own for thirty-two days, nothing but tubes and your own shit to keep you company; what it is to bite into a pillow all night so people can't hear you screaming? No TV, I didn't even have a quarter to buy myself a paper. I tried to get right with your God, I asked him for some spare time, to keep me from pitching my guts every hour, to keep me from shitting all over myself, to give me the strength to wipe my ass good enough so I didn't have to smell myself all night. I prayed that they would stop experimenting on me, stop the rashes, the infections, the sores up my ass. I prayed Mama for some company. I prayed that somebody would get their room wrong and happen into mine so I could talk to somebody, maybe they would even put their arms around me 'cause I was so damn scared, maybe it would be somebody who would come back, somebody who would want to know me for who I really was and I prayed harder and I prayed to your God that if I could just hold on, if I could just get home . . . I'm not going to apologize Mama for loving who I loved, I ain't even gonna apologize for getting this shit, I've lived a lie and I'm gonna have to answer for that, but I'll be damn if I'm gon' keep lying, I ain't got the energy. I'm a deal with it just like you taught me to deal with everything else that came my way . . . but I could use a little help, Mama . . .

[REBA: No more. You hear me Wendal? No more. I never thought I'd see the day I'd be ashamed of you, that I wouldn't even want to know you. (*She exits.*)]

WENDAL: (*Quietly to himself.*) Well, welcome home Wendal.

Body Politic
Steve Murray

Scene: A private school for boys
Serio-Comic
    Patrick: a teacher, 40s

Here, Patrick addresses the student body on the subject of kissing.

O   O   O

PATRICK: An hypothesis, gentlemen. Saturday night. You ask: "May I borrow the car, Dad?" Not, "Can I" but "May I."Can anyone tell me why? Yes, Mr. Marshal, you *may* . . . "Because Strunk and White says so." Not good enough. The difference between Can and May. Anyone? . . . Yes, Mr. Jacobs, correct: the question of permission. "May I kiss you," or "Can I kiss you?" Fear not, gentlemen, this is a lesson in English usage not lovemaking. However, you may learn something not only in politesse but how, as you would put it in your charming hormonese, *to score* . . . All right then, Saying goodnight to the young lady on her parents' porch: "Our revels now are ended." The play, Mr. Gordon? Very good "The Tempest." Imagine your Miranda. The end of a perfect evening at the enchanted Drive-in built by Caliban on the edge of the lagoon, and now, 'round midnight, you linger with Miranda on Prospero's windswept porch. Can you kiss her? Of course. Without asking. Why bother if your sole intent is to smear your lips against hers. Caliban can do that. They did it in the Dark Ages, gentlemen, in the Bronze Age and the Stone, your Paleolithic kinfolk seizing their distaffs by a clotted hank of hair and – ah, l'amour . . . Settle down, gentlemen. You *can,* obviously, kiss her. As the stronger sex. But to ask "May I" signifies not only momentary gallantry, but genuflects to the bloody battles our ancestors fought to forge our polite society. It's a social contract. "May I kiss you" or "can I kiss you." I entreat you, my friends, to memorize the difference, for this is no mere late-night smooch, but the very bedrock of the world of men.

Body Politic
Steve Murray

Scene: A private school for boys
Dramatic
    Scott: a writer visiting his old alma mater, 30

Scott, a recovering alcoholic, has chosen to return to his prep school and confront Patrick, his former teacher and mentor upon whom he had a terrible crush. Here, he reveals his thoughts and feelings to Patrick.

O   O   O

SCOTT: [No, I appreciate your position.] When I moved to New York I was still in the closet. Have sex with your eyes closed, it doesn't count. And I could pass. Very chin-up, purposeful walk. Like they tell you to walk in the city, in case you're being stalked. But the only thing stalking me was me. Until one day it was like a door opened, like walking out of a lifelong twilight.

[PATRICK: New York is New York.]

SCOTT: The years I lived in this dorm, your apartment here at the end of the hall. Your door, regulation puke-green like any other door. But open it, and enter this divine torture chamber. The tutorials you gave. One-on-one. On this couch. Sitting so close. This boiling, my rib cage a cauldron.

[PATRICK: (*Closing the door.*) This is inappropriate.]

SCOTT: All the hours wasted on things I already knew: dangling participles, modifiers. Acting dumb so I could stay a minute longer. You must have known. So bright in class, but an idiot by twilight? Then it happened. Senior year. Out of the blue – because by then, all the time I'd spent walking the quad at night, telling myself I was over these *glandular imperatives.* "If only the right girl came along." Then one night, here on this couch. We were talking college acceptances. Columbia or U.V.A.? You even gave me a beer – against regulations, very buddy buddy. And I kissed you. Climbed on top of you like a hungry puppy. Embarrassing. And you pushed me off, I hit the floor like a drunk. Jesus.

[PATRICK: This –]

SCOTT: You didn't say anything. Worse than death, the silence. You walked to the door, your back straight. I could see what real humiliation meant. Dignified and silent. You would open the door, wait for me to get up off the floor. Only you didn't. You reached the door and you locked it. You shot the bolt and put the chain on and took off your shirt.

Careless Love
Len Jenkin

Scene: Here and now
Serio-Comic
    Jacky: a wanderer, 20s

Following several years of drifting, Jacky returns to his former lover's apartment and discovers her sleeping on the bed. Here, he greets the sleeping woman and proceeds to "catch up."

O   O   O

JACKY: Place looks fantastic, man, really nice. That blue in the kitchen is . . . . Hey, you finally got rid of those plastic milk crates, got yourself an actual bookcase. Two years, it's all changed. Everything but you, and the front door key.

I know I been gone awhile, but hey – I'm back. Some ramblers out there never get home. One guy wasn't even found in his coffin. His old lady opened the box to see his face one last time, and he was gone.

Well, let's see. I don't owe the bank ten big ones on a Buick, and I'm not breaking rocks to make house payments. I live alone, very clean and very simple, and I get by.

I still got my health – most of it.

I been wading in some deep water, but I believe I have reached the shore. Enough said.

. . . Yeah, I been working. Off and on. I am currently participating in a little janitorial venture with the Shrine Circus. They need fifty guys, 'cause the place got ten thousand seats, two shows a night and there's thirty minutes to clean between shows. Everybody gets a mop and a bucket and you hit the aisles. You're not *in* the show, and you're not *watching* the show, you're *in between,* mopping out cotton candy, crackerjax and dead hotdogs at three bucks an hour . . . and looking for lost treasure. I quote my colleague, Big Buster: "Man, this job is the best. Ten thousand people, one of 'em gonna drop a wallet every time."

Lorenzo? Worse than ever. Endless drug deals, that crippled monkey, his passion for pathetic young women, his insane tips on the Tokyo stock market . . .

He's been out about three months now . . . but you can't actually *talk* to him. He's too crazy. Ever since he began hearing those voices, man. Hearing 'em is one thing, but Lorenzo listens.

That's why he tried to take that bank, walking in there with a shotgun bigger than he is, ain't even loaded. Voices told him he was God's own criminal. He's supposed to take his medicine, so the voices don't tell him to do something else. He is not a compliant patient. However, the little bastard continues to function. Smart as ever, in that same ugly way. I try to stay as far away from him as possible. In the next universe.

[Sings.]
It's so cold in China
That the birds can't hardly sing
It's so cold in China
That the birds can't hardly sing
All my hard luck and trouble
Li'l darling, they don't mean a thing . . .

Two years – since that morning you asked me to leave. I was crying, and then you were crying – and then I just got out of here. What was I supposed to do? Argue with the lady? You were right anyway – you always were.

You're still the only good thing ever come round my door. All the rest is a bubble, float away somewhere, light as death.

Just a shadow on the air.

Careless Love

Len Jenkin

Scene: Here and now
Serio-Comic
> Spin Milton: a middle-aged lounge singer, 40-50

Here, a road-weary lounge singer raps with the audience.

○   ○   ○

SPIN MILTON: . . . Briarpatch Lounge. I'm Spin Milton, and this is my lovely ex-wife Marlene. That's just a label. The label on the bottle, not the juice inside. And as most of you out there already know we're the DREAM EXPRESS.

Tonite means a lot to me. It's kind of our anniversary. We've been at the Briarpatch for exactly three months now. Three pretty terrific months. Isn't that right, Marlene?

[MARLENE: Some kind of wonderful . . .]

SPIN: You know, only a few of you out there know this, but I was raised in a state orphanage and after that, an endless series of foster homes. For me, the late night crowd that pulls in here off Central for a little warmth, a little musical sharing – is the only real family I've ever known.

A little musical sharing . . . You know, sharing is caring. Total sharing is total caring. Hey, the truth is you can say it all in three little words. God – Love – Acid. Hey, just kidding. Those days are gone, right – but not forgotten.

Thank you all, a very real thank you, for being with Marlene, and me, and our music.

This is Spin Milton, reminding you again, in case your mind is a little fried, a little shaky tonite – a nite where the outlines blur, things slide into one another – that hand resting on the thin rayon fabric of her skirt, touching the warm thigh beneath, that hand just dissolves into her flesh, flesh to flesh. A meltdown.

Cross-Dressing in the Depression

Erin Cressida Wilson

Scene: Here and now
Dramatic
   Old Wilder: a nostalgic, sensual, ironic and melancholic old man

Here, Old Wilder shares a special memory of his mother.

O   O   O

OLD WILDER: My mother had the most beautiful freckles dripping down her fingertips, streaming down her back, in a waterfall of human brown dots. Some red. Her hair was red, and as we took naps together (It was our favorite thing to do together.) I'd sleep on my stomach, and in my sleep I could feel her hand moving through the sheets, ripping freckles off the surface of her skin. The freckles would fly around her palm, falling like snowflakes onto my skin. She'd spread them across my back, spreading constellations and stars and universes all over me. A map to the moon. By the time I'd wake up, the bed would be full of freckles. We'd be submerged in them, dripping off the bed. Plunk. Plunk. Plunk. I'd hear them dripping in my sleep one by one onto the floor. I wake with a start. I open the sheets and leave. I have grown up. I am covered in freckles. I've been in the sun for years now and I slept a few nights since then too . . .

The Darker Face of the Earth
Rita Dove

Scene: A plantation in ante-bellum South Carolina
Dramatic
　　Augustus: an educated slave, 20s

Augustus has lived an unusual life. He first belonged to a sea captain who treated him as his own son. During those years Augustus was able to travel the Atlantic and Caribbean, learning what he could along the way. He has since been purchased by a plantation in South Carolina where he tells his fellow slaves the story of the violent uprisings that gave birth to the Republic of Haiti.

〇　　　〇　　　〇

AUGUSTUS: When I was in Martinique,
I heard tell of an event
that changed the fate of our people.
Did you know there are slaves
who have set themselves free?
Taken over the land they used to
harvest for others? Shall I tell you
how they drove out their white masters
and forged their own nation,
a nation other nations –
white nations – respect?

[SCIPIO: (*Almost afraid to ask..*) How?]

AUGUSTUS: Santo Domingo, San Domingue, Hispaniola –
three names for an island rising like a fortress
from the waters of the Caribbean.
Mountains jut from the sea so steep,
it seems at first there's no place
to set a ship. But if you go
through the Windward Passage and on around
the northwest coast, you'll reach a place

where the land descends to sea
like a giant stone staircase
and there you can land.
An island like most islands,
with more than its share of
sun, wild fruit, mosquitoes . . .
and slaves, half a million –
slaves to chop sugar, slaves
to pick coffee beans and serve
their French masters in all the ways
we serve our masters here.

(*He motions for the other slaves to move in closer, and they do so.*)

One summer, news of a revolution
in the old country
threw the French masters into a sweat.
Each gruesome outrage, each possible consequence
was discussed evenings as they leaned
back in their rocking chairs
and slaves served the tall cool drinks.
The slaves served carefully,
but listened with even greater care
to talk of a common people rising
against their rulers. The people of France
had marched against their King,
and as they marched they shouted
three words: Liberty, Equality, Fraternity.
Three words were all the island masters
talked about that summer,
and all summer their slaves
served drinks and listened.

One night a group of slaves
held a secret meeting in the forest.
Eight days, they whispered,

and we'll have our freedom.
Lightning flashed in the hills: Equality.
For eight days tom-toms spoke in the
  mountains:
Liberty, the tom-toms whispered.
Brothers and sisters, the tom-toms sang.
On the eighth day, swift as lightning,
the slaves attacked.

[(*Unseen by the others, Amalia enters and stands listening.*)]

To the sound of tambourines and conch shells
they came down the mountains. They swept
onto the plantations carrying torches
and the long harvest knives, the machetes;
they chopped down white men like sugar cane
and set fire to farmyard and manor.
All the whites who could
boarded ships and fled to America.
For three weeks the flames raged.
When the sun finally broke through
the smoke, it shone upon
a new black nation, the nation of:
Haiti!

(*He pauses and looks intently at the faces around him.*)

Now do you see,
brothers and sisters,
why they've kept this from us?

The Ends of the Earth
Morris Panych

Scene: Here and now
Serio-Comic
    Frank: a man on the edge, 40s

Frank is a quiet man who writes a column on gardening for a free newspaper. Following a minor exchange of words with someone who refuses a copy of the paper, Frank is reminded of his early interest in insects.

O   O   O

FRANK: *How* can you not want it?! It's *free*, you idiot! What could be more desirable than a free thing?! The whole *concept* here is that you want it because it doesn't cost anything. Or have you missed the entire point of this, you great, pompous – tit! (*By himself.*) Good God. What's happening to me? I've never lost control like that before. It's the stress of this – this – the pressure of this – *thing* following me – this – but *really*, it's just hard to believe that a free newspaper could have circulation problems. I suppose people are overloaded with information now. And you begin to discover that life is like a big rock. You don't necessarily want to turn it over and see what's underneath. Unless you're an entomologist, that is. Did I mention that I studied insects once? In college. It seemed like the natural field for me. There are a few exceptions, of course, but generally I like insects. If nothing else for their sheer numbers. With insects, there's always a crowd. But I gave up the study when I realized that most people in the field of entomology seemed to end up in the extermination business. It felt rather self-defeating. So I began to write poetry on the subject, which proved vastly unpopular but did give me a feeling for literary composition. I turned to writing fiction next. But that never really worked out. My style is rather – lifeless. I can't even tell a joke, without everybody becoming – sort of – concerned. So I began writing about gardens. I can't imagine there being anything so perfect as those. To look at a garden you wouldn't know what's really going on. So much quiet dignity concealing so much seething underground insect activity. And after all, my name is Gardener. Well, what else would it be? For so long I *tried* to avoid becoming one. If I didn't know better I'd say my whole life had been plotted out for me, like carrot seeds. In neat little rows. "Say. Whatever happened to Frank *Gardener*?" "Gosh, I wonder." There I was. At *The Free Advertiser Weekly*. A gardening columnist. It wasn't much, but I suppose it was something.

The Ends of the Earth
Morris Panych

Scene: Here and now
Serio-Comic
   Walker: a man suffering from paranoid delusions, 40s

*Walker has convinced himself that a stranger is following him with the worst of intentions.
Here, this most paranoid individual describes his very unlucky life.*

○   ○   ○

WALKER: (*Calmly taking out his notebook, he slowly makes note.*)
Definitely – up – to something. (*Putting away the notebook.*) But
why? (*He slowly picks the lettuce off.*) People don't go through my
garbage for no reason. Interview my neighbours. Publish secret
messages in the press. Taunt me with mocking tongue gestures.
Throw salad. (*He rises and begins a journey, as the scene changes
around him again and again.*) These are no accidents – these little
– events – in my life. From that day I was struck by lightning, three
years old, charred and dazed, staring up into the sky and
wondering what happened, I began to sense a certain something
about myself: that I was a sort of – a conductor – of bad things.
You know? That all the ill will that could exist in the universe was
somehow attracted to me, drawn down through me like a kind of
a lightning rod. Just this – lone tree on the landscape. An orphan
from birth, left standing, just waiting for bad luck to strike me.
Sometimes it only happened in little, quiet ways. The way ice
cream falls off the cone. Just another dream lying on the ground.
Melting in the gutter. Or sometimes in ways more excruciating.
Those prospective parents at the orphanage? Looking at me. Ugly.
Ridiculous. Standing at the other end of the room. They'd never
pick me. But how many times did they bring me out anyway, just
to let me know. How many teachers would ignore my raised
hand? How many prayers at night go unanswered? How many
women charitably smile at me in bars. Hoping I wouldn't come

over to chat. How many years pass me by – and how many chances – before I realized there was a kind of pattern to all of this. Life had always seemed to me a little like Bingo. You know: You keep playing, even though someone else is always winning. You don't think about the person calling the numbers. But then, you start to wonder. Gee. How many times can a guy possibly lose? How much bad luck? Bad timing? Bad news? Three broken engagements. Nine broken bones. Four laughable attempts at corrective surgery. One accidentally removed kidney. Three times attacked by animals at a wild game preserve (all in the same day). Five times fired. Eight, laid off. Bingo. Bingo. Twice electrocuted. Once loved. Accidentally. She thought I was someone else. So she says. For two weeks. I didn't know she was supposed to meet him on the corner. I happened to be there. Can you believe it was two weeks before she finally used his name? I can't. I went and lay down in the middle of the road. A car swerved and hit another car. Two people were seriously injured. Bingo. I once fell out of a small airplane on takeoff. Or was I pushed? Just rolled across the runway. And somehow into a cargo hold, unconscious. Flown to Resolute Bay with a consignment of medical supplies. Coincidence? Well, that's what they'd like you to think, isn't it? These people. The ones *he's* with. The ones calling all the numbers. The numbers that are never mine. These are my numbers here. (*With lottery ticket from wallet.*) See. Every week I buy another lottery ticket, just to prove I'll never win. And I never will. I know it with the loss of every job. With every eviction. Every jail term. Oh, yes. Even that, on occasion. You see, I've finally become what they intended. Over time. Lost my . . . civility, you might say. But then, how many lousy numbers can they call, before a guy finally goes after the caller?

[(*Music interlude, during which we see Frank and Walker follow each other. Following this sequence, Walker stands, suitcase in hand.*)]

WALKER: Of course, I shouldn't expect people to really care. After all, isn't life complicated and difficult enough? Yeah – maybe. But *why* is it so complicated and difficult? Well. That's just the way the numbers come up, you think. Bingo. Nobody bothers to think about it.

[(*The scene changes a little so that we see a repeat of the first bus stop scene with Frank, now from Walker's perspective.*)]

And then by chance, one day standing at some bus stop, you happen to notice a stranger who somehow seems connected to something. Something of which you are a part. However unwittingly. He *seems* to be alone. Acting on his own. You might almost *believe* that he's just some nobody – just like you – working away at some pointless kind of – life. Maybe this *isn't* about anything, you begin to think, waiting for your bus. Maybe there *is* no higher order to things. No conspiracy of any kind. Just some runaway machine we're part of. Pistons wildly pumping, the speed accelerating, and no one at the controls. But then, out of the corner of your eye – you may suddenly catch a glimpse of the truth.

Entries
Bernardo Solano

Scene: The Amazon rain forest
Dramatic

Jorge: a young man who has ventured into the jungle on a spiritual quest, 20s

After spending a month or so in the jungle, Jorge is beginning to gain insight into his life. Here, he contemplates his life in the United States as he waits for night to fall.

○   ○   ○

JORGE: July . . . who cares what day it is.
(*He looks at his bites.*)
Chewed me up like a piece of raw meat. No wonder there's no history down here, the ants are always making off with the archives. Termites making mulch out of books, maps. That's why we have so many revolutions, there's nothing left to remind us how badly the last one went. We may as well be ants and termites. All we do is continually clean house. Take apart what somebody else put together.
(*He gets up, looks at the ground.*)
They're all gone. Carried off by other ants, other termites. We don't bury our dead anymore. We eat them. (*Beat.*) I almost wish they had made off with me. My entire life would just . . . disappear from memory. Like I'd never existed.
(*He is standing over the stream.*)
My babbling brook. What do you have to say for yourself, hmm? (*Looking more closely.*) Hey, little fish. Where are you off to? (*Noticing at his feet.*) Dead ant. Left you behind, did they? (*Dropping ant into stream.*) Here you go, little fish, breakfast. . . . Geez, you were hungry, weren't you? Want some more? (*Picking up ant.*) Hey, look, got a live one here.
(*He inspects it between his fingers, changes his mind, gently puts it back on the ground, watches it scurry off.*)
Sorry, little fella.

(*He notices a shaft of sunlight; he holds his hand inside it.*)
Beam of light . . .
(*Notices another, steps underneath it.*)
Hello, sun. Ray of warmth. (*Steps under another.*) Ray of hope.
(*And another.*) Light for the lost.
(*Just as it's becoming like a dance, the sunlight goes away.*)
Damn. (*Beat.*) I'm on that beach again. Why doesn't my father just
swoop down and scoop me up onto his shoulders? Where is he? I
babble something in Spanish and I start to cry. To run. I'm on fire.
A burning boy, burning with fear, with shame, surrounded by a
sea of strange faces. Lost, begging to be found. (*Beat.*) Fit in.
Change the way you dress, walk, talk. Honor society, debate team,
student government. I wasn't any of those people I pretended to
be. But the really scary part was that if I wasn't any of those
people, then who was I? (*Beat.*) I haven't mentioned that I came
back to Columbia once before. A few years back. My Spanish
sucked, I was instantly branded the Gringo. My own relatives took
great delight in pointing out all my North Americanism's. They
didn't know how right they were. The flip side is that I looked
around and I saw families who looked like mine. Who acted like
mine. My upbringing hadn't been so strange after all. But I'd
already spent my first twenty-odd years blaming myself for feeling
out of place, for being different. I was my own worst racist.
(*Long pause. As he prepares to wash his hands and face in the
stream.*)
I keep expecting the ground to open up and swallow me whole.
Makes it tough to be optimistic, you know?
(*He washes.*)
I ask permission of this place…this place of emerald shadows…
(*He washes.*)
Water. Give my dreams life . . . give my life dreams. (*Pause.*) The
day has passed. I anticipate the coming darkness. No one will
protect me.

Floating Rhoda and the Glue Man
Eve Ensler

Scene: Here and now
Dramatic
    Barn: an artist searching for love and healing, 30s

Barn's mother was killed by a wing that had fallen off a statue of an angel. Since that day, wings have become the central theme of his art. Here, Barn does his best to explain his obsession to the woman he loves.

O　　　O　　　O

BARN: (*Pointing to his painting with a pointer stick like a teacher.*) What is a wing Rhoda? Please, think about it. I need you to think about it. I need you to think about wings. A wing is not a muscle per se or a bone. It's a collection of feathers, a mass of feathers glued together, well merged together, inseparably working, blending, flapping to make flight. To make take off. Feathers like waves washing over one another, washing over and over and up and up. Wings are for rising. They carry you. And yet, I was standing next to her on the sidewalk, my mother. It was Valentine's Day and she was wearing bubble gum colored lipstick and hippie heart shell earrings and she was laughing. She was definitely laughing. I was walking funny, five year old funny, trying to make her laugh because her laughing was like a window opening. We were laughing together and then just like that she was falling and it was falling, the cement wing, all broken off, all falling through the sidewalk, through my mother. Mommy. Mommy. I kept looking up Rhoda. Wondering where it had come from, who sent it, praying they would take it back. Secretly hoping another would land on me so I could go with her. Wings Rhoda. We're all missing our wings. It's this invisible hunger for wings that makes us behave like this.

The Gate of Heaven
Lane Nishikawa and Victor Talmadge

Scene: A hospital room
Dramatic
Kiyoshi "Sam" Yamamoto: a Japanese-American veteran of WWII, 60-70

In 1945, Sam was a soldier in the 522nd Artillery of the 442, a division that helped to liberate Dachau. On that day in April, Sam saved the life of Leon Ehrlich, one of the many thousands of prisoners set free by the allies. Years later, the two men meet again in the United States and become best friends. It is now 50 years after the day that fate brought them together in Germany, and Leon is dying in the hospital. Here, Sam pays a final visit and gives his old friend a very special gift.

O   O   O

SAM: I brought you a gift today, Leon.
(*Sam takes out of his coat a small box.*)
I thought about this and told Ruby what I was going to do and she agreed it was a good idea. So, don't you, engyo. You know what that means, Leon, don't you hold back. I guess you're the last one I should think would hold back, huh? (*Sam holds up his silver star medal.*) It's my silver star. (*Pause.*) It saved me, many a time. Whenever I felt like the world was coming in at me, I just took it out and held it. It gave me a lot of strength. I just thought you might need some of it's warmth too. I thought maybe, some of those days when I couldn't get down here, you could take it out and, think about your buddy.
(*Sam pins the medal on Leon's chest. He gently lifts Leon up from the chair and slowly carries him to the bed. For a moment, it mirrors the image at the beginning, at Dachau. Sam puts Leon down and covers him with the blanket.*)
Don't worry, Leon. I got another one at home. Remember, I got Steven's silver star. Funny, huh? Like father, like son. And I have this . . . (*Sam takes out the mazuza from underneath his shirt. It is on the same chain as when Leon gave it to him.*) . . . to think of you.

Grace
Doug Lucie

Scene: England, the present
Dramatic

Rev. Neal Hoffman: an American evangelist, 50s

Rev. Hoffman and his entourage have arrived in England with the intent of purchasing Hartstone, the home of a missionary family and sight of a supposed miracle. Here, the reverend entertains Hartstone's skeptical owner with the story of how his miserable life was saved by the Lord.

O   O   O

NEAL: Well. (*Beat.*) I didn't realize at the time, but what I had was a hunger. I swallowed everything . . . booze, grass, acid, and still I was starving. I had no father to respect; I had no respect for anything or anybody, myself included. I ran around spitting hatred everywhere, round and round, confused, angry and deeply, deeply unhappy.

[RUTH: And then, don't tell me, you found God.]

NEAL: No, Ruth, no. What I'd found was the Devil. (*Beat.*) He spoke to me. I went around in a dream for I don't know how long, with the Devil speaking to me, on and on and on. And do you know what he was saying? (*Beat.*) He was telling me to kill. Yes, to kill. So I went out and I bought a gun. I didn't know who I was going to kill, it could have been the President, it could have been the check-out girl at K-mart. (*Beat.*) But I found myself in a huge stadium. I didn't know why I was there, what was going on, I only knew I had to kill. Surrounded by thousands of people, but who? And then I knew. There he was, framed in lights. There was the man I was going to kill. (*Beat.*) Dr. Billy Graham. (*Beat.*) I had my hand on the gun in my jacket pocket as I pressed forward to get close enough. And the Devil was screaming at me, and Billy was preaching, and I had these voices, yelling and hollering, fighting for my soul. And Billy was telling us to come forward to Jesus, and I was going forward, and I had the gun in my hand. And at last I stood before him. And I was shaking, Lord I was shaking. And then I looked up. (*Beat.*) And the Devil was gone. No more yelling in my head. For the very first time in my life, I felt peace. Complete, silent, loving peace. So I tore off my jacket and threw it way behind me. I fell to my knees. And I said, 'Dr. Graham, forgive me, but I came here to kill you.' And he smiled, and fell to his knees and we prayed together. (*Beat.*) A miracle. (*Beat.*) And that was when I understood. It was me that had to change first. Only then could I change the world.

The Harry and Sam Dialogues
Karen Ellison

Scene: Here and now
Serio-Comic
    Harry: a man searching for meaning in his life, 30-40

Harry's marriage is on the rocks. Lack of communication is the primary source of their marital woes as can be seen when Harry erupts in a stream-of-consciousness tirade following a shopping expedition.

O   O   O

HARRY: Look. Don't ever embarrass me in front of the Safeway! You're out 'a bounds here! You're way out 'a line! I was just making the ride a little smoother. Picking ya' up from work. Taking ya' shopping. Picking ya' up from shopping. I was just making conversation. And some people would find that interesting – the answer to all our problems: the idea we could stuff all the garbage in the world into a black hole, and it would disappear. See, we'd all have underground tunnels in our backyards, and they'd connect at NASA and then NASA would shoot our garbage into space! Into black holes, the universe's garbage cans. That's what they are, Marge! That's interesting! Marge! Marge? That's great. That's just great. I know. Don't tell me. I know. Look. You're the one who wanted to talk. Marge! So now you're giving me the silent treatment. That doesn't make sense, Marge! That's not whadddaya'-call-it. So let's just talk! Or maybe I should say, "dialogue." Dialogue. Where do ya' get these words? And when are ya' going to learn to drive? Okay. All right. So we were having a conversation. Okay. You were talking about your job. Again. Putting up with your boss. How ya' have to deal with all this garbage from your boss. See! See! Garbage! That's where I got the idea! That was the connection in my mind! See how that works! That's interesting! Marge? People have to work sometimes! I do my best. What is wrong with you? I'll tell ya' what's wrong with you. Ya' gotta house. Ya' gotta beautiful fence

37

I built myself for you. For you. But you're not happy with that. Ya' got some idea from some ladies magazine or one 'a your friends that there's more. That something's missing. Well, there's not. This is it, Marge! This is the house, the fence, me. I'm doing my best. I do my best. (*Pause.*) We talk and talk, and we never get anywhere. Did ya' buy Fritos? (*Harry looks in the grocery bag, reaches in and pulls out a box. He opens it and a long string of condoms falls from his hand. Long pause. Harry looks into the bag again.*) Scott! (*Harry takes out a roll of toilet paper from the bag.*) Look at this! Will ya' look at this! I hate this toilet paper, Marge. I hate it. Ya' never buy the brand I like, for Christ's sake! And who's this guy, Scott, Marge?! I mean why is the toilet paper named after a man! What does that mean? And look, there's a pink bow around his name. Scott! Who is Scott, Marge? (*A door slams off-stage.*)

The Harry and Sam Dialogues
Karen Ellison

Scene: Here and now
Serio-Comic
>Harry: a man searching for meaning in his life, 30-40

Driven by loneliness and despair, Harry's wife has turned to his best friend, Sam, for love. When Harry realizes that his neglect of Marge has pushed her away and cost him a friend in the bargain, he makes an honest effort to mend his ways. Here, he runs into Sam at their favorite watering hole and does his best to say that he doesn't want to throw away 20 years of friendship because of one mistake.

○　　　○　　　○

HARRY: Say ya' gotta glass in front of ya'.

[SAM: I gotta . . . (*Harry stops him.*)]

HARRY: And ya' reach for it thinking this glass 'a milk – it's going to go so well with this Ding-Dong I'm eating. This glass 'a milk – it's gonna hit the spot, know what I mean? [(*Sam nods his head yes.*)] So ya' take a sip, and it's orange juice. There's orange juice in your cup, and you were expecting milk. Ya' had the taste of milk in your mind and your mouth before ya' drank, but it's orange juice really there in your mouth now, and it's a shock. And the strange thing is ya' poured it yourself. Get my point? [(*Sam shakes his head no.*)] Ya' think ya' had one thing – the thing ya' wanted, the thing that fit perfectly with where ya' were at the time – milk and a Ding-Dong – but ya' weren't thinking at all. See, all ya' had was an idea, not even words in your brain. Until the shock, ya' had reality blocked out – 'cause what ya' really had sitting right there in front of ya' was something different, something less, something ya' poured yourself not five minutes before, but something ya' didn't really want. You had your own mistake. So I ask ya'. Whaddaya' do after eleven years, twenty years? Spit it out? (*He shakes his head no.*) Swallow it. Pour again. (*Harry pours Sam some beer. Sam laughs. Harry laughs a little, too.*)

The House on Lake Desolation
Brian Christopher Williams

Scene: A hospital room, 1969
Dramatic
    Dorian: a man in trouble with the wrong people, 30

Dorian's best friend has informed him that the mob wants him dead. Before he takes it on the lam, he pays a final visit to his comatose grandmother in the hospital.

O   O   O

DORIAN: Grandma? (*Beat, a little louder.*) Grandma?
(*He puts the pistol on her swinging meal tray as he gently puts his hand on hers. He stares at her for a while.*)
I'm here, Grandma. (*Beat.*) How are you feeling? (*Beat.*) You look very pretty. (*Sighs.*) Did you eat anything?
(*He goes to a blank piece of paper posted on the wall. He shakes his head. He turns back to her. Silence.*)
Were you awake at all last night? That's alright, Grandma. I'll just sit here with you and hold your hand.
(*He does.*)
You have nice hands. Delicate. Delicate little stitches by delicate little hands. Vibrant red roses on a sea of white lace. The bedspread you made me? Possessions never really meant anything to me. But that bedspread. Sentimental value, that's what Mother says. I wonder if she got that from you.
(*Beat.*)
"Be careful what you wish for, Dorian." Remember that? A million years ago, at your house on Lake Desolation, we sat out on your porch. One of those hot nights. There was lightning in the sky but no rain. Heat lightning. Remember? I wanted to be one of the fireflies we were watching that night. "Oh, Grandma, I want my butt to light up." I thought the world could be mine if only I had a rump that glowed. "Be careful what you wish for, Dorian." And you told me about the curse of Aurora and Tithonus. Aurora was

40

so afraid of Tithonus dying that she asked Zeus to make Tithonus immortal. Her wish was granted, but Aurora forgot to mention that she wished for Tithonus to be immortally young. So he lived on and on and on and she was cursed to watch as nature shamelessly robbed him, first of his beauty, then of his health, and finally of his mind. Cursed. Curse-ed. (*Beat.*) I wanted excitement, Grandma. I wanted to know the people in your *Glamour* magazines. (*Beat.*) Mother has to take care of you, Grandma. I know she will. Don't you worry. Someone will always be here with you. I'll always be here with you; I just won't be around, you know, anyplace that you can see me. Charlie's going to disappear and I guess that's . . .

(*He gets up and starts pacing.*)

"Think happier thoughts, Michael." Remember? Peter Pan? Will you say goodbye to Mother for me? I don't really have time and I wanted to see you and . . .

(*His attention turns distractedly towards the bathroom.*)

Everything will be alright, Grandma.

(*His attention jolts back to her but then seems to dissipate.*)

You were always there for me. I hope you can hear me. I want you to know that I know. You were always there for me. I'm letting you down. Maybe I should have gone to computer school after all, hunh? Joined the Navy? Learned a valuable trade. Done something with my life? Maybe.

(*His attention again goes back to the bathroom.*)

Grandma, I have to . . . um . . . I'll be right back.

(*He picks up a hand-held mirror that is beside her bed and enters the bathroom. He leaves the door ajar as he speaks, and we can see him cutting lines of cocaine and snorting. He will return from the bathroom during the following.*)

The curse of Tithonus. It always amazes me how you know these things. For Christ's sake, whoever heard of Tithonus? Or Lady Astor's horse? Did you make that one up? "All dressed up like Lady Astor's horse." You always used to say that. Well, I'm sure you still say that . . . when you're not . . . in a coma. (*Laughs.*) "Life doesn't slow down and it doesn't back up." You always used to say that, too. Jesus, Grandma, when it comes right down to it, you never really shut up. This is probably the first good rest your jaw has had in years.

(*He takes a long look at her.*)

So delicate.

(*He goes to her and brushes her hair.*)

I'll tell you a secret, Grandma. Don't tell anyone now. "Loose lips sink ships." I'm pretty confident you didn't make that one up. I'm going back to Lake Desolation. You know, my hands look like yours. How come I never noticed that? Your hands used to scare me. The veins are so pronounced. They'd be so easy to cut. It used to terrorize me to watch you peel vegetables. One slip of the knife, and . . . I don't want to go away. I want to stay with you.

(*He walks to the window in order to scope outside. He turns back to her.*)

Have you found the answer, Grandma? I'm too young to die. I know that. It has to be true. I don't even know what the question is yet. Have you found the answer?

(*He crawls into the bed with her and holds her.*)

I can only stay just a minute. I have to go. I have to go away. I have to find the source. Have you seen it? When you're done peeling away, is there anything at the core? Oh, Grandma, help me.

(*The lights fade to Blackout.*)

Hysterical Blindness and Other Southern Tragedies That Have Plagued My Life Thus Far
Leslie Jordan

Scene: Here and now
Serio-Comic
>Leslie: a Southerner on his way to Hollywood, 29

Years and sit-coms later, Leslie suddenly finds himself longing to return to the South. His experience as a television star has provided him with the insight that has finally made it possible for him to embrace his homeland along with all of its quirky characters and imperfections.

O   O   O

STORYTELLER: I'll let you in on a little secret. I was kind'a looking forward to moving back to the South. Who'd a thought! I worked so hard to put all that behind me, but does one ever really forget from whence one came? I miss soft, summer nights. Fireflies in the air. Sitting in the porch swing listening to the latest church gossip . . .

[CHOIR MEMBERS: *Bless us! Don't press us!*
Take care how you address us!
You'll see though, that we know
How to make you feel at home.

Ever-present, ever-pleasant . . . we shall never wane.
We are Southern, we are special.
Try to shame us, try to tame us . . . it will be in vain,
See, It's Just The Way We're Bred.
Endearing, never fearing,
And forever persevering.
We're gracious, tenacious,

And we love our Home Sweet Home.

Sing Alleluh!
Keep Smilin' Through!
You'll knock 'em dead . . .
It is Just the Way You're Bred!!!]

STORYTELLER: . . . I miss chicken and dumplings. Anything cooked in gravy. Iced tea with lots of sugar. Oh God I miss cornbread with no sugar. I miss big, fat butts covered in polyester combing the aisles of K-Mart lookin' for them blue light specials. I miss being around people who were raised the way I was raised. To believe in God. To say my prayers at night. To have respect for my elders. Yes ma'am. No sir. People who realize the importance of good manners. I'm almost 40 years old, people, and I still ask to be excused from my mother's dinner table. Please! Thank you! These are important words!

But what I miss most about the South and what my journey out of the South has taught me is that the South has an important, unspoken, tradition of encouraging and nurturing it's eccentrics. When I tell a fellow Southerner that my mother once closed her eyes and did not open them for two years, they don't find that odd. They usually try to top me. *Hell, I had an aunt who used to crawl up on the roof with her Chihuahua dog and howl at the moon.* Or, *my Grandpa once went to the outhouse to shit and the pigs ate him.* I know of no place on earth that breeds such rampant lunacy!!! And we must thank God for that. Or we wouldn't have Tennessee Williams plays. Faulkner novels . . .

[CHOIR MEMBER #4: Eudora Welty short stories . . .]

[CHOIR MEMBER #2: The genius of Truman Capote . . .]

[CHOIR MEMBER #3: Miss Tallulah Bankhead . . .]

[CHOIR MEMBER #6: Hank Williams . . .]

[CHOIR MEMBER #1: Patsy Cline . . .]

[CHOIR MEMBER #5: And Miss Dolly Parton . . .]

STORYTELLER: Dolly! What would we do without Dolly! And I don't think that I would be the person that can stand before you today and pridefully boast. I was born, I was bred and I will die . . .

Southern to the bone . . . crazy as an ol' bed bug . . . and queer as a three dollar bill . . . It's just part of my life. So . . . the good Lord willing . . . if the creek don't rise . . . if mama's eyes stay open . . . you'll glance up at the boob tube and there I'll be . . . just trying my DAMNDEST to let my little Southern light shine out here in a city of BIG LIGHTS . . .

John Dory
Craig Wright

Scene: The middle of the Pacific Ocean
Dramatic
    John Dory: a young man lost at sea, 20-30

John has been lost at sea for nearly four years. He finally manages to climb aboard a small boat inhabited by Mary, a young woman who has been drifting for nearly as long. Here, John tells Mary his story.

O   O   O

[MARY: OUT OF THE BOAT. I WON'T LIVE FOR YOU.]

JOHN: Mary, I want you to eat me and live!

[MARY: Don't bother talking, I can't hear you, LA LA LA LA LA LA LA LA LA LA LA LA LA LA LA LA LA LA LA LA LA LA LA LA.]

(*She opens her eyes and points fiercely at the ship in the distance.*)

[MARY: (*Suddenly focused.*) IT'S THAT SHIP!]

JOHN: What about it?

[MARY: THAT SHIP IS THE PROBLEM, DON'T YOU GET IT?! I don't want to live with a ship like that around! I can't do it anymore! Always wishing, always hoping, it's breaking my goddamn heart!]

JOHN: Mine too! Mine too! Mary, you do this thing for me, and that ship . . . ? That ship becomes immaterial. Let me tell you something?

[MARY: As long as it's not personal.]

JOHN: Alright. Fine. I'll tell you about somebody else.

[MARY: Someone who means nothing to you.]

JOHN: Gotcha.

(*We hear far-off thunder roll across the sky. She looks up hopefully. The sky darkens a bit.*)

JOHN: Once . . . there was this guy. A real regular guy. A sailor. His name was Thomas Dowd. [(*Mary looks at John.*)] And his ship, the Katherine, burned at sea, and then it sunk. But he survived, with a bunch of other men, in a longboat. He held the sticks in his clenched fist when they all drew lots, to see who'd be first to die.

That would always be his job. Because he was a real regular guy. After a long time, and a lot of funerals, this . . . guy, Thomas, found himself alive in the boat with only one other man: the first mate. He didn't like the first mate; nobody did, because the first mate was the Captain's son, but the first mate didn't know anything about the sea, or about sailing, or about anything. The first mate hadn't even really lived . . . then. All through the voyage, the crew had tortured or tormented the first mate, they beat him, they tried to make him rape this slave girl they'd picked up in the Marquesas . . . they made him stay in the crow's nest all night, every night. And the Captain never said a word. The first mate begged to go home, to be let off anywhere, but the Captain insisted, he said, "You're my son. You'll be my first mate. Be a man." Anyway, in the longboat, the first mate told the strangest thing to this guy, Thomas. He told Thomas that HE, the first mate . . . John Dory . . . had set fire to the boat, because he was tired of being treated like dirt by everybody . . . and that all the men who had died, including the Captain . . . had died strictly because of him. These two had watched SO many people die. Ugly deaths. Deaths without dignity. Animal deaths.

(*Thunder cracks closer. Lightning flashes in the sky far off.*)

The first mate offered to kill himself, because he felt bad. Very, very bad. About what he'd done. He offered to kill himself, to do away with the drawing of lots and just kill himself so at least this other guy, Thomas . . . could survive. But Thomas, the guy who this story is about, he didn't want that, he didn't want any part of it. He said to the first mate, "I'm gonna break so many hearts in my life, John, I'm gonna lose count. I'm gonna shit on people left and right. I'm gonna think almost exclusively about myself. I just know it. It's the way I've been, it's the way I'll be. So keep your goddamn flesh and blood, because I don't want it. And I don't want it on my record. You did what you did, now live with it." I argued with him about three more minutes and he threw me out of the boat.

[MARY: So you're John Dory.]

Julie Johnson
Wendy Hammond

Scene: Hoboken, NJ
Serio-Comic
    Mr. Miranda: a self-absorbed teacher, 40s

When a student approaches him for romantic advice, Mr. Miranda automatically (and incorrectly) assumes that the young lady has a crush on him.

○   ○   ○

MR. MIRANDA: I think I know who this person is.

[JULIE: *(Brightening)* Yeah?]

MR. MIRANDA: This person likes you very much, Julie. And is attracted to you. Finds you very attractive.

[JULIE: *(Ecstatic.)* Really?]

MR. MIRANDA: And has actually, often, thought of you in the same way, but to confess, as a confession, I once had a romance with, an affair, I guess, I guess you'd have to call it an affair, with a student, an adult student like yourself and I hurt this student badly and my wife, well, she cried, well, she still isn't over it and I'm not either, I still ask myself every morning when there's shaving cream all over most of my face which makes my eyes stand out very clearly in the mirror, I ask my eyes clearly standing out from the shaving cream every morning how I could have done such a thing to my wife.

[JULIE: Mr. Miranda?]

MR. MIRANDA: Students and teachers just shouldn't fall in love with each other. Well it happens. It does happen. But it's not really the teacher a student falls in love with. She's actually falling in love with the subject matter. And sometimes a teacher seems bigger than life – But when I'm not teaching I'm just a normal boring person. Take my word for it. When I'm at home not teaching I'm really very boring. I even bore myself.

The Kentucky Cycle
Robert Schenkkan

Scene: A rude cabin in southeastern Kentucky, 1776
Dramatic
   Michael Rowen: brutal patriarch of an American family, 35

Michael has carved a home for himself out of the Kentucky wilderness and has kidnapped a young Cherokee woman with the intention of making her his wife and mother of his heir. When she tries to escape, Michaels severs the tendon of her heel, so that she can never run again. Here, he takes a moment to contemplate the violence with which he has forged his life.

O   O   O

MICHAEL: I been killin' as long as I can remember. Ireland. Georgia. Here. Never for the pleasure innit, ya understand – though I'm good at it, and a man should take pride in what he does well. But if you go simple with blood you can lose your way. And I meant never to do that. I was always headed somewheres better. I killed my first man when I was seven. A bloody lobsterback. One o' them that was runnin' our piece of Ireland like his own bloody vegetable patch. They'd have "hunts" on the land, see. Our land. Racin' through our fields on their fine horses in their blacks and scarlets. A beautiful sight! If you could just forget it was your crops out there bein' trampled underfoot for their sport.
(*Beat.*)
Did you ever notice how like the distant bayin' of a fine pack of hounds is the sound of a hungry child cryin' hisself to sleep?
(*Beat.*)
One of the silly bastards had too much to drink and lagged behind the rest. He failed to clear a wall and took a bad fall. His horse rolled over him. Must've broke him all up inside, 'cause he couldn't move none. I got to him first. I stood there, over him, and I remember him lookin' up at me with the queerest look on his face. What a sight I must've been: little snot-nosed, barefoot boy, more dirt than clothes. I wondered what he thought now; him and

his kind always bein' so high and mighty. And then I stepped on his neck and broke it. Like St. Patrick crushin' a snake.

(*Beat.*)

But there was no sport innit. See, I learned early, blood's just the coin of the realm, and it's important to keep strict accounts and pay your debts. That's all. And now here, at last, I'm a man of property meself, on the kind of land ya only dream about. Dirt so rich I could eat it with a spoon. I've but to piss on the ground and somethin' grows. I've corn for whiskey and white oaks for barrels to put it in and a river to float it down and sell it. I've everythin' I've ever wanted: the land, and to be left alone on it. I'm richer than that snot-nosed boy ever dreamed he'd be. But somethin' isn't right.

(*Beat.*)

I'm gettin' in and layin' by more food than one man could eat in a year. And instead of feelin' full, I feel empty. I feel *hungry.* What's the point, after so much blood and so much sweat, if ten years after I'm gone, the damn forest covers my fields again? Or worse, some *stranger* does? Will I have built all of this for nothin'? For no *one?* Michael, me boy, what you want is a family. And for that, you need a *wife.*

(*Star limps over slowly to the table and ladles out stew into a bowl for Michael. For the first time, we notice a clumsy, bloodstained bandage wrapped tightly around her right ankle and calf. Finished serving, Star starts to cross back. Michael stops her with a touch. She freezes instantly. He looks at her leg.*)

Still swollen some, but gettin' better. It'll heal. I cut the tendon cleanly. You'll always limp, but you'll walk soon enough just fine. No pain. But you'll never be able to run. Not fast enough. Not far enough.

(*He releases her. She crosses back and stands by the fireplace. She stares at him as he talks. He raises his glass.*)

Here's to our first born. A *son!*

(*Beat.*)

Gimme a daughter, and I'll leave it on the mountain for the crows.

The Last Time We Saw Her

Jane Anderson

Scene: Here and now
Dramatic
      Hunter: an executive, 60s

During a conversation with an employee, Hunter reveals his prejudice and ignorance.

◯   ◯   ◯

HUNTER: You know what it is, Fran? I think that people are losing their manners. And I mean that in a larger sense. For instance in business, it used to be, if there was a dispute, there was a protocol for sitting down and talking things over. But now, people just pick up the phone – and I'm not a prude, but when someone uses foul language with me it just puts me in the wrong frame of mind.
[FRAN: Uh-huh.]

HUNTER: And here's another example: my oldest daughter, Melissa, works for a law firm downtown. And at lunchtime she goes to a certain coffee shop and there are some individuals who work behind the counter who are consistently rude to her. Not just rude, mind you, but outright abusive, turning their backs on her when she tries to talk to them, giving her evil looks – and by the way my daughter is one of the nicest gals you could ever meet. Melissa calls me in tears and says, "Dad, I just don't understand it." And frankly, neither do I. These particular individuals happen to be black and I don't mean to sound prejudiced, in fact I've hired a lot of black individuals and some of them were very fine people – but I've noticed a general hostility coming from that particular group that's very disturbing. I want to sit down and say to them, "Look, if you really want things to change, then you're going to have to learn some manners." That kind of behavior is just plain counterproductive. Is that being racist?
[FRAN: Uh, well.]

HUNTER: Or maybe it's just being old-fashioned. I don't know. The world is going too fast for me. I wish my daughter could have grown up in a gentler time. There's no reason that she should have to fear for her life when she goes to lunch, absolutely no reason.

Later Life
A.R. Gurney

Scene: Boston
Serio-Comic
    Austin: a man on Prozac, 50s

Austin has been reunited with Ruth, a woman with whom he had a fling 30 years earlier. Here, he tells her of his divorce and the depression that followed.

○   ○   ○

AUSTIN: (*Laughing.*) Maybe so. (*Pause.*) Anyway, it doesn't work. Psychiatry. At least for me. It may work for them – the younger generation. They're so much at home with all that lingo. And they're all so aware of their own feelings. I mean, they strum on their own psyches like guitars. So it probably works for them. I hope it does. After all, their life is ahead of them. But me? Even if I . . . could say . . . even if I found some way of . . . I mean, it's a little late, isn't it?

[RUTH: Don't say that. You should never say that.]

AUSTIN: Anyway she hasn't a clue. My psychiatrist. Not a clue. I sit there in this hot room on Copley Square, overlooking Trinity Church, trying to explain. But she hasn't the foggiest. It was all so different. The world I came from. It was a totally different culture. All those . . . surrogates. That's what she calls them. Surrogates breathing down your neck. Nurses. Cooks. Maids. Gardeners. Aunts and Uncles. Parents, too, of course. And Godparents. Grandparents. *Great*-Grandparents, for Christ sake. All this pressure. Vertical and horizontal. You were like a fly caught in this very intricate, very complicated spiderweb, and if you struggled, if you made a move, if you even tweaked one strand of the web, why the spider might . . . (*Pause.*) Anyway, what does she know about a world like that? My shrink. She grew up in a cozy little nuclear family in some kitchen in the Bronx.

Life Sentences
Richard Nelson

Scene: Here and now
Serio-Comic
Burke: a literature professor, 40s

Here, Burke describes his first meeting with Mia, the woman he loves.

O   O   O

BURKE: Politics is coming back. (*He sips his drink.*) You can just feel it. It's in the air. *I* think it's because people are beginning to care again. It is caring itself that is coming back.
(*Beat.*)
Politics *and* caring. (*Smiles.*) It will be great. It'll be . . . (*He is lost in thought for a moment; suddenly he smiles to himself and laughs:*) They can push us liberals around only so long. And then! (*Laughs.*) Then . . .
(*Short pause.*)
If you wait long enough for something. If you only have the patience – . It will be great. (*Starts to sip his drink, but stops.*) I say this to Mia – . Mia's my – . We're a couple. We're not embarrassed to see ourselves as a couple.
(*Beat.*)
I'm not. So I say this to Mia. That politics I think is coming back. And she says, "Don't tell me about it." (*He laughs a little too hard:*) Women! (*Laughs, then stops and tries to correct himself:*) Not all women. I didn't mean – . In fact in a lot of things women are just as – . Most things. In really probably just about everything. In fact, I think women are probably better than men in every – . Just better than men.
(*Beat.*)
This is one thing we've learned in the last twenty years.
(*Beat.*)
I've learned it.

(*Short pause.*)

I wasn't making fun of Mia. Not that she'd mind. She's got a great –. I was joking. She was joking.

(*Forces a laugh.*) She's very funny. When I first met her – . Well, it took about two years of living together before I was sure she wasn't all the time putting me down. She has that sort of sense of humor. (*Laughs.*) For example, she tells everyone the only reason she moved in with me was because I had a house and the school system in Dutchess County isn't so bad. (*Laughs.*) She has a daughter – that's what the bit about the school system was referring – . Anyway, you get the sort of sense of humor. (*Shakes his head.*) She's funny. And it's all done with an absolutely straight face. (*Laughs.*) She's subtle.

(*Laughs. Pause. He sips his drink.*)

We met in a restaurant. (*Gestures: "like this one here."*) A bar/restaurant. The bar part of a restaurant. In the Village. I was completely taken with her. One look and it was . . . I said to myself – Burke, you could fall for this one. Really. And I have never said this to myself before or since. Amazing.

(*Beat.*)

And she was taken with me too. I learned this later.

(*Beat.*)

I learned this about four or five years later. Suddenly it just all of a sudden came out of her. "Burke," she said, "remember that first time we met? You know I was really taken with you." I was stunned when she said this. I thought she was joking! (*Tries to laugh.*) Anyway, even though she tries to hide it, I think (*Whispers.*) that Mia is almost as far to the Left as me. You cut through that tough – . What's inside – . The caring, the feeling . . . She's quite instinctive about all this. Like that, she cuts through the shit. On social issues, I mean. Domestic – . As for foreign policy – . She doesn't read newspapers, so – .

(*Beat.*)

Newspapers, it's sort of a thing of her's. A conviction, you could call it. That's what she calls it. Not to read newspapers. At first I thought she was joking – . But – .

(*Beat.*)

She means it.

Love Allways
Renée Taylor and Joseph Bologna

Scene: Here and now
Serio-Comic
    Tony: a man suffering through a mid-life crisis, 40-50

Driven by feelings of guilt, Tony here confesses his feelings of love for another woman to his wife.

O   O   O

TONY: Nothing happened. Nothing! (*He starts pacing.*) Alright, I'm going to tell you exactly what happened. It started yesterday afternoon. I asked her to go shopping with me to pick out a birthday present for you. So, we met in the lingerie department at Saks. She didn't even look particularly good when I saw her. She wasn't dressed up; white tight pants, T-shirt with no bra, and her mink. That's all. So, I don't want you to think she had anything in mind when she met me there. She was as innocent in all this as you and I are . . . Well anyway, she modeled a beautiful negligee that she thought you'd like. She just sort of wrapped it around her, and started striking different poses. Well, who comes walking into the lingerie department but Nancy Bowden. So, Phyllis started laughing nervously. Later, she told me in the elevator that Nancy probably thought that we were having an affair, and she caught me buying her a negligee behind your back, which we thought was very funny at the time. (*He laughs nervously; she stares.*) In the elevator . . . and you would have, too, if you had been there. I mean, it's not so funny now, but it was in the elevator . . . So, we went for coffee, and we giggled a lot. Mostly she giggled. I just sort of got a kick out of her giggling, you know? . . . And that's all that happened. And I didn't give it another thought, until last night when we all had dinner. I don't even know why I asked her to dance. I mean, I didn't think anything was going to happen, or I never would have asked her. So, anyway, I put my right arm around her back, and with my left hand I took her hand. And when her hand touched my hand, I felt a strange sensation go right through my body and hers. Tell me if you ever felt this with anyone on the dance floor, It was sort of a quiver and a tingle that starts in your toes and goes right up to every nerve ending in your body. It's not sexual. It's more of a total sensation of overall pleasure. Did that ever happen to you? (*She starts to answer, but he continues.*) And then we started dancing. I spun her out. And then I pulled her toward me, and our bodies came together, and that's when it happened . . . I mean, nothing was really happening except we were just standing there holding each other, and the feeling was that I just wanted to stay there and hold her forever. I mean, we didn't even say a word, but I knew she was feeling the same thing. I sensed it from her sighs, and the change in her breathing, and once in a while she let out a couple of deep moans . . . So, that's it, Ruth. That's what happened . . . Ruth, I'm really scared. I can't make it without you. You're good. You're kind. You're smart. If you were me, what would you do now? Just tell me, and I'll do it. No questions asked. (*She starts to say something.*) Alright. The simplest thing would be to just sweep everything under the carpet . . . No, that's no good. Because, for the rest of my life, my body would ache for Phyllis and I'd start hating your guts . . . Alright, look . . . You love me, and I love you, right? I suggest I see Phyllis with your permission, but I don't do anything. I just keep feeling that feeling with her, and we see where it leads. (*Suddenly he stops pacing and speaks with great difficulty.*) Ruth . . . I'm sorry, I've got to be honest with myself and leave you and marry her . . . Wait a minute. If I marry Phyllis, we'll both feel all kinds of guilt about hurting you and Johnny, so, the question is, "Can this great feeling I have for her withstand all that?" I mean, how long do you think it would last with her? A night? Two nights, a month, two months, three months? Okay, maybe a great no holds barred love affair. Three months of sex, and laughing and good times and total bliss. And then what? I'd probably have the same trouble with her after being married for twenty-three years that I'm having with you . . . Then what do I do? Run off and marry someone else? What kind of life is that?

Twenty-three years with this one. Twenty-three years with that one?

So, forget Phyllis. I got a feeling this is bigger than me and Phyllis. This is bigger than me and you. This is profoundly about man and woman; the concept of male/female relationships itself. Look, in certain cultures, a man has eight, nine wives at the same time. One he talks to, like I'm talking to you. One he gets a big sexual charge from, like I got from holding Phyllis. One's a gourmet cook. One loves sports. So, maybe that's it, Ruth. Maybe I've got to reach out to a lot of beautiful, sexy women who turn me on. What do you think? (*Before she can speak.*) Damn it, that's not going to work. I know you. With your sense of fairness, you'll want to have a lot of men . . . Look, maybe I could sexually experience a lot of women without having to sleep with them. I mean, maybe I just have to hold them and dance with them, because now that I've felt that feeling, I've got to keep feeling it, or I'll lose my mind.

You know, I didn't tell you this, Ruth. The day before yesterday, I sat in Battery Park watching all the women walk by, and I started writing this song: (*He sings softly.*) "Beautiful girls, beautiful girls,/I love to sit watching those beautiful girls/in straight hair, or curls,/those beautiful girls go by."

So, what do you think? . . . I know, it stinks. But, what the hell do you want? I never wrote a song before. I never had a nervous breakdown before either. Maybe I just want to have the adolescence I never had. Maybe if you help me through my adolescence, everything will get back to normal with us. While I'm holding and dancing, you can take up a hobby . . . or travel . . .

Look, what's the use? If I run around madly in love with a lot of women or just one woman, eventually I'll want to have sex with them, and our marriage would end. And, I do love you, even though it's not the way I want to. I'll have to settle for that. So, that's it. The decision is made. We stay married, and somehow I'll get these thoughts out of my head. We're stuck with each other. This may blow over in a few days. If not . . . well, I've always resisted therapy, but maybe you could help me find a psychiatrist who specializes in feelings of total deprivation. Come on, let's go to bed. I feel so much better now. I'm sorry I brought the whole thing up. Good night. (*He starts to get into bed, but suddenly stops and jumps up.*) Wait a minute! What the hell am I talking about. I don't need therapy. I know what I need. I need to feel what I felt with Phyllis. I want to stay married to you, so I need it from you. That's it! That's the answer! No more living only for the kids, or our careers, or our favorite causes. (*He grabs her.*) Dance with me! (*He holds her tightly.*) I want to be madly in love with you! I don't care how long we're married! I want it to be like it was with us in the beginning! I have to be madly in love with you, Ruth! I can't hold back anymore! I just can't! (*He begins to cry as he continues to hold her tightly.*) I love you so much, Ruth. I'd die without you.

Mambo Quasimodo
Steven Tannenbaum

Scene: Here and now
Serio-Comic
    Man: a hunchback with a Lenny Brucesque point of view, 30s

Here a deformed man reveals an interesting if sad aspect of his relationship with his father.

O   O   O

MAN: My father . . . (*He takes out a pill bottle, shakes out a fistful of pills and swallows them.*) . . . My father has a finely-tuned bat sonar system that never failed to detect me when I was about to approach his sector. No. let me amend that statement a bit. His sonar system was so highly developed it could actually alert my father even if I was just thinking about approaching him.

I would hear the TV in the den, so I'd make my way downstairs and by the time I got there – it took me a long time – the den was dark, the TV was off and my father was long gone. Then I'd hear some noise in the tool shed. And I'd think; that's what happened. The man's had a sudden and uncontrollable urge to be with his socket wrench. So I'd muster up my energy again – I wasn't so light on my feet back then – and head for the tool shed. By the time I reached the shed, the door would be padlocked and there'd be no one in sight. No matter how fast I tried to move – which wasn't that fast – my father always managed to stay one room ahead of me.

Then one day, my mother and I drove out to my father's plant to pick him up after work. We waited as a wave of burly men carrying black lunch pails came streaming out the gate. Finally, I spotted him. My father was with a couple of other workers, laughing it up, as a cigarette bobbed up and down at the end of his lip. At that moment, above the din, I heard my father's name. Some guy was running after him, calling out his name.

So my father stopped and waited. He waited. He waited for the man to reach him; and when he did, my father enthusiastically slapped him on the back. It's not that I had a conscious epiphany at that moment; but my child's mind registered and filed away that incident for future mining.

Mambo Quasimodo
Steven Tannenbaum

Scene: Here and now
Serio-Comic
    Man: a hunchback with a Lenny Brucesque point of view, 30s

Here, the hunchback discusses the death of his mother.

O   O   O

MAN: (*Still recovering, slowly returns to his room.*) It's always the one's you like who die. You know, John not Paul; Bobby not Ted; Buffy not Jody . . . My mother not my father. But I suppose if my father had been the one who died, then he'd be the one I like.

It's been so long since I've seen her, I'm almost certain that she's just a figment of my imagination. All I can conjure up now are inert flashes of grainy history that remain separated by miles of barren grey matter. Sometimes I am dogged by truncated images that have been permanently detached from their original context. This is what I see: barefeet in thongs. One foot juts out to the side. The other is pointed straight ahead. I would like to imitate that image but my body does not go that way.

I wish I could remember a whole day spent with her instead of isolated moments. Actually, the strongest memory I have is the one everybody said I would forget. In an instant, without the slightest bit of effort, I can picture my mother in her hospital bed languishing like a blow-up doll. My father had brought me there because "mommy had something important to tell me."

When I got there, I sat in a very big chair that was way across the room. After I had been in the room for a while, my mother pressed the button that made the head of her bed rise. She had wanted a clear view so she could motion me to her side. I wasn't scared so I walked right up to her. She smiled and said something but it came out all garbled. I turned and said, "Daddy, Mommy talks funny." My mother grabbed me with her bony fingers and moved me so I was facing her once more. Again, she said something but I couldn't understand it. I noticed her eyes were all full of water and I thought her voice sounded liquidy, too. Then my mother put my hand in hers, brought it to her lips and kissed my palm. Her lips were dry but the water from her eyes dropped onto the tips of my fingers. Whereupon, my father nudged me and said, "Kiss your mother and say good-bye." . . . "Good-bye Mommy."

My father promised me that after a while I'd forget the bad memories and only remember the good ones. But the good times happened before I knew I was supposed to remember things. Besides, how can a kid's memory compete with intravenous tubes and his mother's haunted eyes. He should have warned me that only the ones you like die; then I would have tried harder to remember.

Medea

Euripides
Translated by Alistair Elliot

Scene: Corinth
Dramatic
   Jason: a man grieving for the loss of his sons, 30-40

*Jason has foolishly forsaken his first wife, Medea, in order to marry the daughter of Creon.
Driven mad with rage, Medea kills their two young sons in a horrifying quest for revenge.
When Jason discovers her crime, he curses her from the palace battlements.*

O   O   O

JASON: You hateful woman, abominable thing,
Loathed by the gods and me and all mankind!,
You could pick up a sword and hack the bodies
Of children you had borne, to leave me childless.
You have done this and dare to face the Sun
And Earth! Oh harsh and sacrilegious heart!
I curse you – now, in my right mind at last,
Not senseless as I was when from your home,
That barbarous place, I brought you back with me
To a civilised land, already evil then.
The avenging demon who was meant for you
The gods have turned on me – you killed your brother,
The boy who shared your childhood: foul with blood
You stepped aboard my lovely boat, the Argo.
So you began; and after lying as a wife
Beside me, after bearing sons to me,
From jealousy and lust you kill them too.
No woman born in Greece could bring herself
To such an act, and yet in preference to them
I chose to marry you, I chose the hand
Of the enemy who was going to destroy me,
A tiger, a savage, not a woman.
Ah, but a million insults could not bite

Into your heart, it is so brazen hard.
Go, monstrous spirit, stained with children's blood.
Out of my sight. Leave me to weep, and rail
Upon the god who minds my destiny:
That I shall never enjoy my new-found bride,
Never hold my sons again in my arms.
All, all; all is lost; I lost them all.

Moonlight
Harold Pinter

Scene: Here and now
Serio-Comic
    Ralph: a former soccer referee, 50s

Ralph's best friend, Andy, is on his death bed. Here, Ralph shares some insight into Andy and soccer.

       O   O   O

RALPH: Were you keen on the game of soccer when you were lads, you boys? Probably not. Probably thinking of other things. Kissing girls. Foreign literature. Snooker. I know the form. I can tell by the complexion, I can tell by the stance, I can tell by the way a man holds himself whether he has an outdoor disposition or not. Your father could never be described as a natural athlete. Not by a long chalk. The man was a thinker. Well, there's a place in this world for thinking, I certainly wouldn't argue with that. The trouble with so much thinking, though, or with that which calls itself thinking, is that it's like farting Annie Laurie down a keyhole. A waste of your time and mine. What do you think this thinking is pretending to do? Eh? It's pretending to make things clear, you see, it's pretending to clarify things. But what's it really doing? Eh? What do you think? I'll tell you. It's confusing you, it's blinding you, it's sending the mind into a spin, it's making you dizzy, it's making you so dizzy that by the end of the day you don't know whether you're on your arse or your elbow, you don't know whether you're coming or going. I've always been a pretty vigorous man myself. I had a seafaring background. I was the captain of a lugger. The bosun's name was Ripper. But after years at sea I decided to give the Arts a chance generally. I had tried a bit of amateur refereeing but it didn't work out. But I had a natural talent for acting and I also played the piano and I could paint. But I should have been an architect. That's where the money is. It was your mother and father woke me up to poetry and art. They changed my life. And then of course I married my wife. A fine woman but demanding. She was looking for fibre and guts. Her eyes were black and appalling. I dropped dead at her feet. It was all go at that time. Love, football, the arts, the occasional pint. Mind you, I preferred a fruity white wine but you couldn't actually say that in those days.

My Funny Jarvik-7
Richard Strand

Scene: Here and now
Serio-Comic
> Joseph: a man with a broken heart, 20-30

Here, the suffering Joseph relates a strange dream about Susan, the woman he loves, to his psychiatrist.

O   O   O

JOSEPH: And then I see Susan.

(*Lights come up on Susan. Backlight only. We cannot see her face.*)

[DOCTOR WYER: Who?]

JOSEPH: Susan.

[DOCTOR WYER: Why does that name ring a bell?]

JOSEPH: (*Quite irritated.*) Susan!

[DOCTOR WYER: Oh, sure. Susan. Susan. You see Susan.]

JOSEPH: Do you know who I'm talking about?

[DOCTOR WYER: Sure. Susan]

JOSEPH: Right. Okay. I see Susan. And I want to touch her. Only when I reach out my hand . . .

(*Joseph reaches out his hand to Susan. Susan reaches her hand out to Joseph. At the moment they touch, Susan falls limp on the floor.*)

 . . . she, she, unravels. Right in front of me. Something goes snap and I hear a sound like fzzzz and then she unravels.

(*The lights fade on Susan.*)

Then I look overhead and I see, you know, telephone wires. And they're, well, they're unravelling. Fzzzz. I hear something go snap, and then I can see, inside the insulation, the wires are unravelling. Fzzzz. Like they've been wound too tight and now, fzzzz, they're unravelling. Snap, fzzzz. And the trees, something inside the bark, it goes snap, and I can see the bark ripple, fzzz, and then the branches droop and the trees fall into a limp heap of lumber. And then the guy, he . . .

[DOCTOR WYER: The plaid shirt guy?]

JOSEPH: (*Desperate to keep the pace going.*) . . . starts to . . . what? Yes! The plaid shirt guy! His shoulder muscle snaps – I can hear it – and I see his skin ripple while his muscles unravel, fzzzz, and his arm falls limp.

(*Marty reaches out his arm which falls limp, apparently victim to unravelling muscles.*)

And then all his muscles snap and unravel. Snap! Snap! Fzzzz, fzzzz, fzzzz. And he falls at my feet, like laundry down the chute.

(*Marty completely unravels and falls into a pile. His lights fade to black. So do Doctor Wyer's. Joseph is alone in his spot.*)

And then me. I hear a snap right here.

(*He points to his shoulder.*)

Snap. Fzzzz. My arm falls limp. It is a fleshy pendulum, hanging from my shoulder. Then snap again, right in my inseam. And my leg unravels. Fzzzz.

Pause. He does not fall limp. He stands alone in his spot. Then he turns and crosses to Doctor Wyer's office. Lights cross-fade as he moves. He lies down on the sofa.)

Then I wake up.

My Funny Jarvik-7
Richard Strand

Scene: Here and now
Serio-Comic
   Joseph: a man with a broken heart, 20-30

Joseph here describes the night he first met Susan, the woman who broke his heart.

O   O   O

JOSEPH: She was sitting at a table across the room from me. Marty was playing the sax. Anything sound familiar yet? It was one of those rare moments, like you only see in the movies. Just looking at each other, we had closed a switch. We knew, just looking at each other, that we were somehow connected. It was almost literally electric. One of those rare, extraordinary moments . . .
(Joseph is lost in his own moment.)
I joined her at her table.
(Joseph crosses to Susan.)
I said to her, "We are connected. We form, somehow, a completed circuit. You feel it too, don't you?"
(Susan turns her head to Joseph. She is silent.)
She asked me to join her.
(Joseph sits next to Susan.)
I said, "It's more than just attraction. Attraction can happen any time, to any mammal. People and cats and giraffes and cows all feel attraction. But we are connected. You feel it too, don't you?"
(Susan gestures toward Joseph.)
I said, "We reside in the same place. Like love and morality; we cannot be separated. You feel it too, don't you?" I said, "There is voltage here. Literal, measurable voltage between us. You feel it too, don't you?"
(Susan slowly rises and exits.)
And she did. She felt it too. But things went bad. And she broke my heart.

(*The lights cross-fade back to Doctor Wyer's office as Joseph returns to the sofa.*)

She broke my heart! What are you going to do about it, Doctor Wyer? She broke my heart!

1969 or Howie Takes a Trip
Tina Landau

Scene: Here and now
Serio-Comic
    Howie: a man remembering his past, 40s

Here, Howie shares an unhappy memory of his first day of high school.

O   O   O

HOWIE: I remember I remember the first day of high school and there we were and the morning was fine and there was no indication whatsoever that in a couple of hours a few people, one person in particular, Curtis Callender to be exact, would destroy my life. I mean why, I always wonder, I wasn't dressed funny I was kinda normal I think looking in fact so why was I immediately an outsider? Curtis, the leader, just stopped me in the hall, looked at me and grabbed me here by the collar and says "hey faggot, what are you doing in our school?" You see the funny thing about it like funny weird not funny ha-ha is that Curtis and I had, up to that point, no contact with each other whatsoever, I mean I may have seen him once in a while around town, but that was it. So that was the first time I heard the word "faggot" but I had to wait until I got to the safety spot of my own house before I could look it up, there's no place like home you know, and there it was, the truth right there in the dictionary: a bundle of twigs. I am a bundle of twigs, I am a bundle of twigs. Incomprehensible to me. Simply and irrevocably and always beyond meaning for me, I mean it was every day in the school year times four for each year of high school that I was called faggot and I mean, can you tell me please how could someone who barely knew me hate me so much? Well you know he's the most popular guy in the school, so you see he popularized this activity, I mean that of hating me, so everyone wanted to get into the act, you know, do the cool thing. That's how my horror began.

A Perfect Ganesh
Terrence McNally

Scene: India, the present
Dramatic
    Walter: the unhappy spirit of a young man killed in a gay-bashing incident, 20-30

Walter's mother, Katherine, is traveling to India on a quest to relieve her feelings of guilt and grief over his death. Here, Walter watches over Katherine from the wing of the airplane and tells the story of his murder to Ganesha, the Hindu elephant god.

       O   O   O

MAN: A car whizzes by. Voices, young voices, scream the obligatory epithets: "Fag. Queer. Cocksucker. Dead from AIDS queer meat."

[GANESHA: Oh dear, oh dear!]

MAN: I make the obligatory Gay 90s gesture back. (*He gives the finger.*) Die from my cum, you assholes!

[GANESHA: Oh dear, oh dear!]

MAN: The car stops. The street is empty. Suddenly this part seems obligatory, too. Six young men pile out.

[KATHERINE: Black! All of them black!]

MAN: No, mother! All of them you!

[MARGARET: (*Loudly, because of the headset.*) I think we saw this movie at Watch Hill.]

MAN: Six young men with chains and bats. One had a putter.

[KATHERINE: Six young black men! Hoodlums! Two of them had records!]

[GANESHA: Oh dear, oh dear! All of you!]

MAN: I stood there. It seemed like it took them forever to get to where I was standing. There was a funny silence. Probably because I wasn't scared. I said, "Hello." I don't know why. I hated them. I hated everything about them. I hated what they were going to do to me. I knew it would hurt. I wanted it to be quick. So I said "Hello" again. The one with the putter swung first. You could hear the sound. Woosh. Ungh! against the side of my head. I

73

could feel the skull cracking. He'd landed a good one. Then they all started swinging and beating and kicking. I stayed on my feet a remarkably long time. I was sort of proud of me. Finally I went down and they kept on swinging and beating and kicking, only now it wasn't hurting so much. It was more abstract. I could *watch* the pain, corroborate it. Finally, they got back in their car, not speaking anymore. They weren't having such a good time either anymore, I guess. None of us were. I was just lying there, couldn't move, couldn't speak, when I could hear their car screeching a U-turn and it coming towards me, real fast, just swerving at the last minute, only missing my head by about this much. What I figure is this: they were gonna run me over but at the last second one of them grabbed the wheel. So they weren't 100% animal. One of them had a little humanity. Just a touch. Maybe. If my theory's right, that is. But that's when you waited to love me, mama.

Perpetual Care
Jocelyn Beard

Scene: Here and now
Dramatic
   James: a man at the end of his life, 60-70

   Here, James visits his wife's grave and tells her that he thinks he is about to die.

O   O   O

JAMES: Mornin', Miss Napierkowski. Looking mighty fine today. Looks like old Chuck was out your way with the weedwacker. Yes, mighty fine . . . uh-oh, you got the dandelions again, Mister Sanchez. I'll get Maria to give Chuck a call. I'd do it myself, but I'm savin' my knees for Emma Mae. (*Pauses in front of a poorly tended grave with a tiny headstone and sighs.*) Little Miss Lottie Lemon, you are in a sorry state. (*Bends with difficulty and clears some debris from grave.*) Don't worry, darlin', I'll get you all cleaned up as soon as I've had my visit with Emma Mae.

(*James rises and approaches Emma Mae's grave. He contemplates it for a moment and then kneels, placing the mums to one side.*)

Good mornin' my sweet Emma Mae. These knees don't seem too interested in doin' much for me today. There. (*Pulls out a bunch of wilted mums.*) Looks like the frost done gave the business to your Halloween mums. Well, I'll tell you a little secret, darlin': I knew it would so I went on down to the Whispering Pines Nursery first thing this morning and let old Clint Foster sell me these fine purple fellas. Let me get these dead soldiers out of there . . . (*Replaces flowers.*) There. (*James leans back on his heels.*) They got the Christmas shop open at Whispering Pines. You remember how the kids used to bug us right on through Thanksgiving to take 'em to the Christmas shop to see Santa Claus? Poor Clint must've thought that the only reason you and me bothered having kids was so's they could sit on his skinny white lap at Christmas time. (*Chuckles.*) He never did fit in that costume. Wendell always knew

– remember? Five years old and he could spot a fake Santa Claus a mile away. (*Pauses.*) He's thinking about leaving the DA's office. Wants to go into private practice with Elise. You warned him, Emma Mae. You told that boy that marrying a divorce lawyer would bring him nothing but trouble. (*Pauses.*) Lysandra's still in Kenya at the Mission. Emma Mae, she seems more and more distant every time we talk. You were the only one she'd ever speak her mind to, and now . . . well, I never was any good with the girls. She's working with AIDS patients – kids. Kids, can you imagine? No, I guess you probably couldn't. You never knew AIDS. You knew enough, though, didn't you, old girl. Your own children put you through it . . . speaking of which, James Junior is doing well – finally. He's been out of rehab for a long time now, and his boss took him off of probation last week. They've reinstated all his privileges and he and Bernice are talkin' 'bout seeing some kinda counselor who'd help them put it all back together. That'd be nice, wouldn't it? Wendy's still with your sister. She's doing good since the stroke and Wendy's a big help. (*Pause.*) The grandchildren are all doing great. Davey's rappin' up a storm and little Tisha assures me that his rhymes are def and stupid. (*James rises slowly and painfully as he continues.*) That's good, I think. The house is fine . . . except that Mr. Jones is moving out of the third floor apartment to go live with his mother in Florida. The neighborhood ain't what it used to be, Emma Mae, and I'm worried that we won't be able to find someone to take the apartment. Wendell's putting an ad in the paper for me. I guess we'll just have to wait and see what happens. (*Pause.*) I've got something important to tell you, Emma Mae. I've been getting these . . . pains, right there (*Touches chest.*). They come in the middle of the night and burn right through me. I haven't said anything to anyone yet. I know, I know: go see Dr. Grant. You always did think that fool could walk on water. Well, I'll get to it . . . but I wanted to tell you first. You see, I have this feelin', Emma Mae. This strange and powerful feelin' that I'm going to be seein' you again real soon. I'm ashamed to say it, but I've never really believed that I would until now. Don't ask me how or why, but when that pain comes into me in the middle of the night, I feel so close . . . so amazingly close to you that all of a sudden I don't really mind the pain. It's like you're holdin' me tight, just like you used to when I first got home from the war. The pain comes and the next thing I feel your arms around me and smell that perfume you used to wear . . . I've been talking to you like this every week for the past 10 years, and this is the first time I haven't felt like a sorry old fool. You know what that tells me, Emma Mae? It tells me my time is nearly up and you're waitin' on me. (*Pause.*) Well, that's all I wanted to say. I just wanted you to know that whatever it is you're doin', it's helping me. I love you more right now than I did that day in the field behind your Daddy's house when we picked all those black-eyed Susan's and dreamed up castles in the thunderheads. (*Pause.*) Good bye, Emma Mae.

(James turns from Emma Mae's grave and starts to exit. He stops by Lottie Lemon's grave and, remembering his promise, cleans the dead leaves away from her headstone.)

(*As he exits.*) Good bye, Lottie Lemon, I'll have Chuck tend to you when he comes out to take care of Mr. Sanchez. Good bye, everyone. I'll see you next week.

Police Boys
Marion Isaac McClinton

Scene: A police station
Dramatic
   Royal Boy: a gangbanger, 14

To prove himself to the Police Boys, a violent gang, Royal Boy selects to rape and possibly murder a woman he has grabbed in the park. Following the rape, Royal Boy is filled with feelings of remorse for the fact that everything nice gets destroyed one way or another. Here, he tells his victim the story of the birth of his son.

O O O

ROYAL BOY: Man, I saw my baby being born, you know? I mean, that shit was great, the best. Old girl wasn't no chickenshit behind it neither. She being nothing but thirteen and she was and she was hard like a motherfucker. I mean, we ain't shit but kids, you know what I'm saying? What the fuck we know? We just hoping and praying and wishing and dreaming, trying to prepare ourselves to deal with a miracle, you know? Me going, "push it, baby, push it, push, push, push, yeah call every kind of dirty motherfucker you want for getting you into this shit, but keep breathing and pushing little momma. Kick my ass but keep pushing. She throwing down like the heavyweight champion of the motherfucking world, all scared and hurting, looking all lost and shit, but battling with all of her heart, man. Fighting with everything she got, and then BOOM!!! . . . there the little motherfucker is you know what I'm saying? I look at him, I look inside of his eyes and I see me, man. I see my soul and shit. Right there, man. I go, "You the man." I tell him, "You ain't gotta worry about shit, I got your back for motherfucking life and shit." Man, it was the first time in my life I felt proud of being me, of being alive. The first time I could remember feeling like I was a human being. The shit was magical, man. You know?
[LADY IN WHITE: Seems like so long ago.]
ROYAL BOY: I went to wash up. I wound up in some room anyways,

I don't know where I'm going, I'm a happy motherfucker this day. I was all sweaty and shit, right? I'm washing my face and this white nurse comes in and throws something in the waste basket and leaves. Man, I don't know why I looked in that basket. But I saw . . . I mean, like . . . aw, shit.

[LADY IN WHITE: What did you see?]

ROYAL BOY: She had thrown away somebody's black baby. Somebody's aborted baby, man. Right in front of me, like she was throwing away a snotted up kleenex or something. She even dumped other shit on top of it, without blinking. Then I looked again in the mirror and I saw the truth, man. I wasn't nothing but a ghetto bastard. Just like that poor little motherfucker in the waste basket, just like my own kid, man. Something that life could throw away without a second thought. Something expendable. Something to go out with the trash.

Pterodactyls
Nicky Silver

Scene: Here and now
Dramatic
 Arthur: a man who has just discovered that his son has AIDS, 50-60

When his wife informs him about Todd's disease, Arthur retreats into denial and memories of happier times.

O   O   O

ARTHUR: When he was a boy, Buzz wanted to be a sports announcer on the radio. He loved the Philadelphia Phillies. He talked about them all the time. He said their names over and over again: Nick Etten and Danny Litwiler, Eddy Waitkus and his favorite, Granville Hamner. Buzz worshipped him. He saw the poetry in his name. Oh, that was me. Not Buzz. I liked the Phillies. Buzz drew a lot. I think. Buzz was born a month after my father died and I was a little distracted. He never liked the Phillies, I did. But later, we had catches, on the yard. And like all little boys, Buzz looked up to me and idealized me. He admired me. He loves me and I love him. He's my son and my world and the most important thing in my life – did I say thing? I mean person. And I would do anything for him. Take any suffering. I would cut off my arm. I wouldn't cut off my arm. I know it's a figure of speech, but I wouldn't. I need my arms. He's not the most important person in my life. I do love him, but I said that, didn't I?

Satan in Wonderland

Ron Mark

Scene: Here and now
Dramatic
    Vinetti: a seasoned detective, 40-50

Dr. Max Ziggerman specializes in the treatment of adult survivors of satanic ritualistic abuse. Max's wife is dying of cancer, and when the patient with whom he is currently working suddenly declares that the cult now possesses his wife's soul, he rushes to the hospital to find that she has died. Max doubts that Detective Vinetti will believe his claim of cult involvement in his wife's death, but here, Vinetti surprises him.

VINETTI: Look, cops know stuff people don't know. Shrinks don't know. Don't want to know. We see stuff. Tongues nailed up on walls. Testicles stuffed into body cavities. Pentagrams – I've seen them, doctor – carved into people's chests. Half-eaten brains in the refrigerator. Tag on it, six, six, six. Stuff a normal human's never going to see. But a cop, you tell a cop we got scumbuckets torturing kids, sacrificing them to Satan, cop's gonna believe you. But a normal human? A judge? A jury? Where's the proof? No body, no case. Where's the bodies?

[MAX: Where's Jimmy Hoffa?]

[(*Janet comes in, stands upstage.*)]

VINETTI: You'd never know by looking at this face, but I read. History. Genghis Khan, King Herod, Hitler? Shit, got every one of them right here in my precinct. Three-year-olds selling crack, turning tricks for their mothers. Mothers selling the kid to teachers, lawyers, senators. Stuff that I see I don't tell nobody, not even my wife . . . You tell me there's a thing inside your patient belongs to a cult that gets off roasting children on a spit . . . [Sorry, lady. The doctor and me, we're . . .]

[(JANET: It's all right.)]

VINETTI: (*To Max.*) I believe you. Kid tells me this, I'm gonna believe him. But walk out into that street there. Stop the mailman, a dentist, a schoolteacher. Tell them what's going on, they're gonna scream witch hunt, and you are the hysterical maniac. Witch hunter, Joe McCarthy. Satanic murders? Take it to Geraldo Rivera or the National Enquirer. 'Cause it's just a fantasy, right? Kids are lying, them women are nuts. Human adults do not murder babies for Satan. A fantasy . . . fucking country lives in a fantasy. Got its head rammed two feet up its butthole. [Sorry, lady . . .] Ain't no cults. Ain't no devil. No mongols neither, no Nazis and Joe Stalin's really Santa Claus . . . Going back to that IC unit. Nail these motherfuckers.

Satan in Wonderland
Ron Mark

Scene: Here and now
Dramatic

    Max: a psychiatrist specializing in the treatment of adult survivors of satanic ritualistic abuse, 40s

    Max's patient, a terrified woman with multiple personalities, warns him that the cult that ritualistically tortured her is too strong for them to fight. Here, Max reminds her that humankind has survived a greater evil than a cult, and will always continue to do so.

    O   O   O

MAX: Ida and Shlomo. (*He crosses upstage to the bookcase, takes the urn.*) Think your family is strange? (*Opens the urn.*) Say hello to Uncle Shlomo. (*Clicks his heels.*) Sondercommando. You know das verd? (*Mock Nazi salute.*)

[KASEY: I don't care to.]

MAX: The grounds were lovely, he told me. Manicured lawns. Three rows of folding chairs for the orchestra. Jewish girls, see. All rosy and pubescent in their white lace frocks, pretty blue ribbons. "The Merry Widow." You know that one. (*He hums it.*) That one. And Ida Goldstein waltzes past the girls with a white towel and a bar of brown soap. Fooled some of them. But nobody fooled Ida Goldstein. 'Course, even the schlmazels caught on when the steel door slides shut and they can't find a faucet or a drain on the floor. That's when they'd hear *Na Gid Ihen Schon Zu Fressen,* which loosely translates to, "Let's give 'em something to chew on." And what they gave them were these lovely amethyst crystals, much like the color of your dress, no?

[KASEY: Yes.]

MAX: No. These pretty little jewels were called Zycon B and they'd float down from the grates in the ceiling like purple blossoms. The music played . . . (*Hums Merry Widow.*) Eighteen minutes on the dot. The steel door slides open, Uncle Schlomo comes in looking like a space man. Gas mask, hip boots, a noose and a hook.

They'd be stacked up in a pyramid, you see, climbing over each other toward the vents in the ceiling. Shlomo, he'd go to work, hook and noose, loading it all onto rail wagons so Sondercommandos could shovel it all into ovens. For this service they gave Shlomo his life, such as it was. But there's a romance interest here. Want to hear it?

[KASEY: No.]

MAX: The Romance Part. Friday, June 24, 1940, the door slides open and there stands Ida Goldstein, holding her towel and soap and bald as a baseball. But one look into Ida's baby blues and Schlomo drops his hook. Drops his noose, walks into the gas chamber, takes hold of Ida's hand, stands there like a shnook. Figures this grand gesture's going to win Ida's heart in a big way. Kosher macho, right? Want to know what she does? What that bald, starved, dying Ida Goldstein does?

[KASEY: What did she do?]

MAX: Zlunk. She slugs him. Slaps his teeth out, ones he had left with no gold. She picks up the hook, picks up the noose, puts them in his hands, says, "Nudnick! Go back." He's crying by now, snot running down his face. "I can't. It's too terrible. I don't want to live." Zlunk. She pops him again. "Do your job," she says. "Live and tell." But Shlomo's just standing there and the SS guard's getting very impatient with all this lachrymose schmaltz. So she plants this tremendous kiss on Shlomo's mouth, right where she hit him. Well, that did it. Shlomo takes his hook and noose, walks out. Now comes the funny part, okay?

[KASEY: Okay.]

MAX: The Funny Part. That night Shlomo bribes a Jewish guard, gives him a piece of mouldy bagel, to let him get into the ovens. The goofy nudnick couldn't stay away from that woman. 'Course, there's no way he could tell her stuff from the rest of it. All that gray dust, cinders, chunks of charred up bones. I mean, when it comes down to basics, down to our ashes, we all kind of speak the same language. Lie there or get blown away by the same wind, same old laws and rules. Same kind of grammar . . . but he did it. He took Ida's ashes and he lived and he told. 'Course, them days, hardly anybody believed him. Human beings do not do human beings like that. But he told and kept on telling 'til the day he calls me into his room, hands me his urn . . . schmaltzy part?

[KASEY: Yes.]

MAX: Schmaltzy Part. Hands me this ugly thing, says, "Maxie, there is something I want you to do for me." "Anything," I says. "Cremate me and mix me all up with the ashes in this urn." So I did it. And here they are . . . and whenever I start believing only the scumbags ever win, whenever I think life's only dying and drooling fits, I unscrew this lid, stick in my finger. Don't take much, see. Little touch here. (*He puts ash on his forehead.*) Little touch there. (*On his chest.*) I can take on giants.

Slavs!
Tony Kushner

Scenes: Moscow, March 1985
Dramatic
> Aleksii Antedilluvianovich Prelapsarianov: A Politburo member of incalculable rank, the oldest living Bolshevik, 90s

Here, a man who's seen it all cautions against radical social and political change.

O   O   O

ALEKSII ANTEDILLUVIANOVICH PRELAPSARIANOV: And *Theory? Theory?* How are we to proceed without *Theory?* Is it enough to reject the past, is it wise to move forward in this blind fashion, without the Cold Brilliant Light of Theory to guide the way? What have these reformers to offer in the way of Theory? What beautiful system of thought have they to present to the world, to the befuddling, contrary tumult of life, to this mad swirling planetary disorganization, to the Inevident Welter of fact, event, phenomenon, calamity? Do they have, as we did, a beautiful Theory, as bold, as Grand, as comprehensive a construct . . . ? You can't imagine, when we first read the Classic Texts, when in the dark vexed night of our ignorance and terror the seed-words sprouted, and shoved incomprehension aside, when the incredible bloody vegetable struggle up and through into Red Blooming gave us Praxis, True Praxis, True Theory married to Actual Life . . . You who live in this Sour Little Age cannot imagine the sheer grandeur of the prospect we gazed upon: like standing atop the highest peak in the mighty Caucasus, and viewing in one all-knowing glance the mountainous, granite order of creation. We were One with the Sidereal Pulse then, in the blood in our heads we heard the tick of the Infinite. You cannot imagine it. I weep for you.

And what have you to offer now, children of this Theory? What have you to offer in its place? Market Incentives? Watered-down Bukharinite stopgap makeshift Capitalism? NEPmen! Pygmy children of a gigantic race!

Change? Yes, we must change, only show me the Theory, and I will be at the barricades, show me the book of the next Beautiful Theory, and I promise you these blind eyes will see again, just to read it, to devour that text. Show me the words that will reorder the world, or else keep silent.

The snake sheds its skin only when a new skin is ready; if he gives up the only membrane he has before he can replace it, naked he will be in the world, prey to the forces of chaos: without his skin he will be dismantled, lose coherence and die. Have you, my little serpents, a new skin?

Then we dare not, we cannot move ahead.

Slavs!
Tony Kushner

Scenes: Siberia, 1992
Dramatic
    Yegor Tremens Rodent: a government official, 50s

When Rodent is confronted by a woman whose daughter has been deformed by her exposure to toxic materials, he sidesteps the issue and tries to woo her political sympathy.

O   O   O

YEGOR TREMENS RODENT: (*Quietly, carefully, furtively.*) Mrs. Domik, may I speak to you, not as a representative of the government but in confidence, as one Russian to another?
(*Little pause.*)
This nation is falling apart. It is the hands of miscreants and fools. The government does not serve the people, but betrays the people to foreign interests. The tragedy of your daughter is but one instance, a tragic instance of the continuance of the crimes of the Communist era through to the present day. Chaos threatens. The land is poisoned. The United States is becoming our landlord. Dark-skinned people from the Caucasus regions, Moslems, asiatics, swarthy inferior races have flooded Moscow, and white Christian Russians such as you and I are expected to support them. There is no order and no strength; the army is bound hand and foot by foreign agents pretending to be our leaders, but they are not our leaders. They stand idly by as the United Nations imposes sanctions and threatens war against our brother Slavs in Serbia who are fighting to liberate Bosnia; the great Pan-Slavic empire has been stolen from us again by the International Jew. Not because we are weak: we have enormous bombs, chemicals, secret weapons. Because we lack a leader, a man of iron and will; but the leader is coming, Mrs. Domik, already he is here, already I and millions like us support him. We need more women. Motherland, Mrs. Domik, is the spiritual genius of Slavic people.

(*Reaching for his briefcase.*)
Would you like some literature?

Stephen and Mr. Wilde
Jim Bartley

Scene: Toronto, 1882
Serio-Comic
    Oscar Wilde: British dramatist, 27

Oscar Wilde has hired Stephen, a black manservant, to accompany him on his lecture tour of North America. Stephen was freed from slavery by the Union Army, and may or may not be wanted for the murder of a former slave owner in Baltimore. Wilde has discovered a book on slavery as well as some radical political pamphlets among Stephen's things which have given him a new insight into the question of rights for blacks. Here, he shares his feelings with Stephen.

O   O   O

WILDE: . . . and it occurred to me suddenly, as I was reading your book – *The Narratives of Fugitive Slaves,* it's called – it occurred to me that you must have quite a history; which I had surmised, of course, but it didn't strike me with real force until last night. You see, here I was, all alone, rather drunk, and with your personal effects and books and pamphlets strewn about me – well I'd invaded your privacy in the worst sort of way – and all at once I was wracked with guilt. And I felt . . . what? I felt insignificant. Your whole history was spreading itself out before my mind's eye. It was composed of fact – the few facts which I know about you – and imagination, and incidents from this book which I was reading. Terrible incidents. One in particular, entitled "Hunted by Men with Muskets." Quite exciting really; but ghastly when one considers that it *happened.* This wretched man was being hunted, almost for sport it seems, although the strictly legal excuse was recovery of property – meaning the man himself – but I saw all of this happening to *you.* It was . . . well, it possessed me. That you'd been bound, chained, worked from dawn till dusk, beaten and spat upon most likely, and finally freed, only to be conscripted into the army, which is another sort of slavery, and forced to participate in perhaps the bloodiest war of the century, in which you no doubt witnessed unspeakable acts of barbarism . . . and yet you survived. And here you are: making better wages than many a white man, able to converse and exchange repartee with highly educated men like myself and, well, if I may be immodest for a moment, travelling with one of the foremost celebrities of the age. You have triumphed, Stephen, through the most hideous adversity, and what have I done? Well, I have triumphed as well, in my own eccentric way, and within the somewhat larger confines of my class. But adversity? My pinnacle of adversity consisted in paying a twenty-seven-pound fine to Magdalen College, for arriving late to the Easter term, because I was on holiday in Greece. (*Pause.*) Oh yes – and I was once dragged through the dust and spat upon by a team of college footballers.

[STEPHEN: Why was that, sir?]

WILDE: I told them that football was all very well for rough girls, but that it wouldn't do at all for sensitive young men.

The Stillborn Lover
Timothy Findley

Scene: A house on the Ottowa River, 1972
Dramatic
   Harry: a Canadian Ambassador suddenly recalled from Moscow, 50s

Harry's secret life has finally caught up with him. A closet homosexual, Harry has served as Canada's Ambassador to Egypt, Mexico, Greece and the Soviet Union. His young Russian lover has been murdered, and Harry is the prime suspect. Here, Harry shares an important moment with his wife and best friend, Marian.

O   O   O

HARRY: Yes. You love me. (*Beat.*) Yes. You love me. (*Beat.*) What a piece of news that was, the first time I heard it! *Marian loves me* . . . (*Beat.*) Not like the first news I had. The very first news I received was that my parents had died. I was six years old. Six. "There's been an accident," someone said. "There's been . . . a terrible accident." (*Beat.*) And my guardian – my uncle said to me: "I will show you how to survive." Stand up straight – stare life in the face – and tell it you have come to bargain for terms. When it says "I want you – just as you are" – tell it "No – not without terms." Negotiate. Diplomacy. Restraint. But I was . . . I was I. Me: hidden. What you have to learn, I discovered, is how to hide out in the open. That was the bargain. Those were the terms. *Don't.* Then I fell in love – a long, long ago – with Francis Oliver. That was when I made my choice. To live incognito. And so, we never embraced. We never touched. I never held him – never. Francis knew, of course – knew that I loved him. I'll never know if he loved me. But he said to me: "You are my stillborn lover, Harry." True. Yes. True. And he went to Spain and died. Leaving me with everything unsaid. Until I met you.
[MARIAN: I love you, Harry.]
HARRY: Yes. And I – dear God, how I love you. But I have been your stillborn lover, too, passing through your life on a diplomatic passport . . .

The Survivor: A Cambodian Odyssey
Jon Lipsky

Scene: The rice fields of Cambodia, 1970s
Dramatic
    Pen Tip: a man struggling for survival in the Killing Fields of Cambodia, 20-30

Pen Tip was once a radiologist but now serves Uncle Mao under the brutal reign of the Khmer Rouge. He obsesses on his fellow laborer, Dr. Haing Ngor, and in a fit of envy, reveals the doctor's identity to the Khmer Rouge. Here, Pen Tip describes Ngor's first round of torture.

O   O   O

PEN TIP: Hear that? On a Honda motorcycle, comes the King of Death. That's what the prisoners call him, the King of Death. He speaks to you softly, calmly, with a smile on his face. He says, "If you live there is no gain. If you die there is no loss."

[KING OF DEATH: If you live there is no gain. If you die there is no loss.]

PEN TIP: He asks, "Were you a Captain Doctor?" If you were a Captain Doctor, he says, "Angka will forgive you. Angka needs Doctors." You say, "Taxi! Taxi!"

[NGOR: Taxi! Taxi!]

PEN TIP: He says, Okay. "If you live there is no gain."

[KING OF DEATH: (*Overlapping.*) If you live there is no gain.]

PEN TIP: "If you die there is no loss."

[KING OF DEATH: (*Overlapping.*) If you die there is no loss.]

(*Sound of motorcycle revving.*)

PEN TIP: He leads you out to a field of crosses. Tied to these crosses are bodies, limp and floppy, dangling from ropes. Beneath these bodies are mounds of rice husks, and the rice husks are burning, burning very slowly.

[NGOR: (*Overlapping.*) Taxi! Taxi!]

[(*King of Death flicks a cigarette lighter. The sound is amplified by the loudspeakers: Flick.*)]

PEN TIP: The King of Death hoists your body up on a cross and flicks his cigarette lighter at the mound of rice husks at your feet. Flick. To your right hangs a pregnant woman begging for her mother. Flick. To your left hangs an old man who has soiled himself. Flick. The fire ignites. Thick smoke swirls about you. The flames lick your feet. Flick. If you live there is no gain. If you die there is no loss.

[KING OF DEATH: (*Whispering.*) If you live there is no gain. If you die there is no loss.]

PEN TIP: "After four days, he takes you down, opens your eyes a crack. Beside you is the pregnant woman lying on her full, round belly. He kicks her over. Rips her blouse. Still, she lies there, very still. He picks up a bayonet and slashes her belly. He pulls out her baby and breaks its neck. Around its neck, he ties a string. Suddenly you know what you saw hanging from the prison parapets, those black shrivelled things. He digs down again and pulls out her liver.

(*He forces Ngor to look at the liver.*)

Hungry?

(*Pen Tip and King of Death exit.*)

The Trap
Frank Manley

Scene: Here and now
Dramatic

   Brady: a professor accused of sexual harassment, 40

When Dr. Brady appears before the members of the review board that will decide his fate, he explains that the incident in question – an alleged sexual attack on a male student – occurred when he had blacked-out from too much alcohol. Since, as he claims, he was not aware of anything happening at that point in time, he feels that he isn't responsible for his actions.

O   O   O

[PITTMAN: Of course, Dr. Brady.]

BRADY: Then tell them to shut up. Shut up, I'll tell them.

[PITTMAN: We take your point – (*Glancing about.*) I'm sure no one will interrupt. Suppose you explain – (*Gesturing vaguely.*)]

BRADY: (*Continuing.*) I was in a blackout.

[PITTMAN: We understand.]

BRADY: I'm not responsible for what I do in a blackout.

[PETRUCCI: (*To Pittman, leaning forward, looking down the table at him.*) I don't understand.]

[PITTMAN: I'm afraid we don't understand, Dr. Brady.]

BRADY: I accept my nature. I have no way of knowing what I might do –

[PITTMAN: (*Interrupting.*) In a blackout.]

BRADY: (*Continuing.*) – if I were no longer in charge of my body. If it went its own way, as it were. I don't think I'd initiate it.

[PETRUCCI: What are you saying?]

BRADY: I might not have rejected him. I have no way of knowing.

[TABOR: He made advances?]

BRADY: (*Shouting.*) I have no way of knowing! (*Regaining control.*) I accept the possibility. I have had a good bit of time to think about it, and I accept the possibility – yes. If I was drunk and didn't know what I was doing – (*Breaking off.*) I saw a movie. A woman making love to a man. She was on top. The man was in a Nazi uniform. She was a Jew or a Norwegian. Just as she was about to have an orgasm, she saw this tattoo on his hand. She knew what it meant. He was the one who had killed her husband. The camera cut to her face. We see the look of horror and disgust. But she can't stop. She keeps on thrusting faster and faster. She throws her head back and moans with pleasure. That's what I mean! – (*Shouting.*) She reached a point where she couldn't help it. Something took over and went on without her.

[THURMAN: (*Interrupting.*) And that's your defense. (*To Pittman.*) That's his defense?]

BRADY: Listen to me. A man has needs. He does what he can to satisfy them. Sometimes it doesn't matter who does it. I'm not talking about gender now. It's deeper than that. It's like a machine. You're out of control. And that just makes it more exciting. I mean the passion. Look at the prisons. Look at the army. They're full of strong men, real men, who get what they want from other men. But they aren't homosexuals. That's important. Get that clear. The ones that do it – the ones that, you know, act as the women – they're homosexuals, of course. The others just use them. I might have done that if I was drunk enough – who knows? If I was aroused enough – who wouldn't? It's perfectly natural. Augustine says it's the most natural of sins. (*Shrugging.*) We're just animals.

(*Long Pause.*)

Trophies
John J. Wooten

Scene: Here and now
Dramatic
David: a young man confronting his feelings for his father, 20

David has never gotten along with his strict father. His visits home from college become more and more strained until it becomes quite obvious that something has to give. During a particularly charged Easter visit, David finally confronts his father with the following observations about their relationship.

O   O   O

DAVID: I was up there getting my stuff together and as I packed everything in my suitcase, ready to storm out of here and never come back, it occurred to me what Bobby and Laura said. How it gets worse for them when I come home. How I use them to get at you. And I sat down and looked around the room I grew up in. I tried to remember what it was like being a little kid. I tried to shut my eyes and force time to reverse, to take a different path. I mean, that's what we both want, isn't it? Time to rewind itself? (*Crosses to Mr. Stone, puts present on table next to his father.*) Anyway, I thought of how my visits home have grown uglier, shorter, and less frequent. I started thinking maybe I've been selfish, maybe what they said was true. I was tempted to unpack the suitcase, run downstairs, and declare I wouldn't be leaving. I was here for the duration, here to save this family! . . . But that would be proving Laura and Bobby wrong. And as much as I hate to admit it and as much as it hurts, I'm afraid I can't do that. And as pathetic as that makes me feel, I don't think I can stop behaving this way . . . You see, when I was sitting up there, I couldn't reverse time, but I could see time. Feel it. Almost like I was there again. I saw a man in front of a television set and he was like a statue, his eyes wouldn't move. And next to him I saw a little boy, very young, and he was speaking to this statue, asking it questions. It was clear he was the boy's hero and the longer the man remained still and distant, the more frequent and desperate the questions became. And his longing grew to such a point that he wanted this frozen hero of his to lash out, hit him, kick him, anything. Anything to let him know he was there, let him know he existed. (*Pause.*) Stupid kid, huh? You and I both know there's no such thing as heros . . . Anyway, I couldn't rewind time. But what I saw made me realize I no longer hate you, Dad. I don't hate you because I don't think I love you anymore.

What Cops Know

Kenn L.D. Frandsen

Based on the book by Connie Fletcher

Scene: A retirement dinner

Dramatic

   Chief/Retiree: a man stepping down from the force after serving for many years, 60s

Here, the Chief closes his speech with some thoughts on murderers.

$\bigcirc$ $\bigcirc$ $\bigcirc$

CHIEF/RETIREE: There always comes some quiet moment when you're standing there with the dead person. And you know that if that murder is going to be avenged, it's up to you to avenge it. It might be some old lady in her seventies – she's lived in the neighborhood all her life, the neighborhood's changed around her, she's been at death's door for the past twenty years – one night they come in and kill her for her few pitiful possessions. And that's the one where you look at her and you say, "This is it. We're gonna get them." Any cop would be a liar if he tells you, "I don't care." The day you can't feel is the day you know you quit. But, you can't take it personal, because then it's gonna affect you. You gotta look at it, it's not nice to look at, but I'm gonna have to look at it, and then you gotta put it in a bag. I had friends killed on the job. That was personal and I did cry. But, if it's somebody else, you have to keep that away. Look, there are evil people in the world. People tell you they're sick, they need help. I hear that all the time. The ones who tell you that – they're sick to think it. People say killers need help. They don't need help, they need to be locked up. The last thing you ever want any killer to know is that you're at a dead end. You want to keep that sphincter puckered. You want to keep him looking over his shoulder, you want to keep him thinking that when that knock comes, they're coming for me. Because if you let them get comfortable, he's gonna figure – "I got away with murder." My thought when I came on this job was that nobody should get away with murder. I still believe that. I just believe – there's a lot of crime that happens, and people get away with crime daily. Nobody should get away with murder. I think if Joe and Jane Citizen knew how bad it was out there, they'd get their family in a rowboat, row out to an island, surround the island with a brick wall, and put cannons all over the walls. People don't realize how bad it is out there. They have no idea. And it's all around. There's always somebody out there trying to beat somebody out of something. Here's another story. You try not to think about it, but you can't stop. You can't shut it off. Tonight, tonight, I'll think of everything, all over again, as I have thought about it every day that I have been a cop. I'm proud to have served on the force. It's my special secret and it's all mine. There are things I can never share, would never share. I tried once with Mik, tried so hard, and then I learned to keep it to myself. Now, there's a little part of it, but you'll never know, can never know. Us cops take our secrets to the grave. (*Takes a long drink.*) Thanks for coming tonight. It means a lot. I'd been waiting so long, so long. So long. Good night.

Permissions Acknowledgments:

foreign languages are strictly reserved. The amateur live stage performance rights to LOVE ALLWAYS are controlled exclusively by Samuel French, Inc., and royalty arrangements and licenses must be secured well in advance of presentation. PLEASE NOTE that amateur royalty fees are set upon application in accordance with your producing circumstances. When applying for a royalty quotation and license please give us the number of performances intended, dates of production, your seating capacity and admission fee. Royalties are payable one week before the opening performance of the play to Samuel French Inc., 45 West 25th Street, New York, NY 10010-2751, or at 7623 Sunset Blvd., Hollywood, CA 90046-2795, or to Samuel French (Canada) Ltd., 80 Richmond Street East, Toronto, Ontario, Canada M5C 1P1. Royalty of the required amount must be paid whether the play is presented for charity or gain and whether or not admission is charged. Stock royalty quoted on application to Samuel French, Inc. For all other rights other than those stipulated above, apply to Bridget Aschenberg, c/o International Creative Management, 40 West 57th Street, New York, NY 10019.

MAMBO QUASIMODO by Steven Tanenbaum. Copyright © 1994, by Steven Tanenbaum. All inquiries should be directed to the author at 440 West 24th Street, New York, NY 10011.

MEDEA by Euripedes, translation by Alistair Elliot. Copyright © 1992, by Alistair Elliot. All inquiries should be directed to Oberon Books Limited, 521 Caledonian Road, Islington, London, N7 9RH ENGLAND.

MOONLIGHT by Harold Pinter. Copyright © 1993 by Harold Pinter. Originally published by Faber & Faber Ltd. Reprinted by permission of Faber & Faber Ltd. and Grove/Atlantic, Inc. All inquiries should be directed to Faber & Faber, Ltd., 3 Queen Square, London WC1N 3AU, ENGLAND.

MY FUNNY JARVIK-7 by Richard Strand. Copyright © 1993 by Richard Strand. ALL RIGHTS RESERVED. CAUTION: Professionals and amateurs are hereby warned that MY FUNNY JARVIK-7 being fully protected under the copyright laws of the United States of America, the British Empire, including the Dominion of Canada, and all other countries of the Copyright Union, is subject to a royalty. All rights, including but not limited to, professional, amateur, motion picture, recitation, lecturing, public reading, radio, broadcasting, television, and the rights of translation into foreign languages, are strictly reserved. Particular emphasis is laid on the question of readings, permission for which must be secured from the author's agent in writing. All inquiries concerning rights should be addressed to the author's agent, Robert A Freedman Agency, Inc. at 1501 Broadway, Suite 2310, New York, NY 10036, without whose permission in writing no performance of the play may be made.

A PERFECT GANESH by Terrence McNally. Copyright © 1994, by Terrence McNally. All rights reserved. CAUTION: Professionals and amateurs are hereby warned that A PERFECT GANESH by Terrence McNally is subject to a royalty. It is fully protected under the copyright laws of the United States of America, and of all countries covered by the International Copyright Union (including the Dominion of Canada and the rest of the British Commonwealth), and of all countries covered by the Pan-American Copyright Convention and the Universal Copyright Convention, and of all countries with which the United States has reciprocal copyright relations. All rights, including professional, amateur, motion picture, recitation, lecturing, public reading, radio broadcasting, television, video or sound recording, all other forms of mechanical or electronic reproduction, such as information storage and retrieval systems and photocopying, and the rights of translation into foreign languages, are strictly reserved. Particular emphasis is laid upon the matter of readings, permission for which must be secured from the Author's agent in writing. Inquiries concerning rights should be addressed to William Morris Agency, Inc., 1350 Avenue of the Americas', New York, NY 10019, attn.: Gilbert Parker.

PERPETUAL CARE by Jocelyn Beard. Copyright © 1994, by Jocelyn Beard. Reprinted by permission of the author. All inquiries should be addressed to Jocelyn Beard, RR 2, Box 151, Patterson, NY 12563.